Developmental Agile Leadership

Developmental Agile Leadership

Empowering Teams in a Changing World

Timothy Kloppenborg and Kam Jugdev

BEP

BUSINESS EXPERT PRESS

Leader in applied, concise business books

Developmental Agile Leadership:
Empowering Teams in a Changing World

Cover design by Cassandra Kronstedt

Interior design by S4Carlisle Publishing Services, Chennai, India

First published in 2025 by
Business Expert Press, LLC
222 East 46th Street, New York, NY 10017
www.businessexpertpress.com

ISBN-13: 978-1-63742-884-9 (paperback)
ISBN-13: 978-1-63742-885-6 (e-book)

Portfolio and Project Management Collection

First edition: 2025

10 9 8 7 6 5 4 3 2 1

EU SAFETY REPRESENTATIVE
Mare Nostrum Group B.V.
Mauritskade 21D
1091 GC Amsterdam
The Netherlands
gpsr@mare-nostrum.co.uk

To our spouses, Elizabeth, and Doug,
for their encouragement, love, and patience

Description

Leaders face many complex and unforeseen challenges as the second quarter of the twenty-first century unfolds turbulently. Leaders need adaptability and agility to meet these challenges. In **Agile leadership**, leaders must make swift decisions, foster open communication, and support their teams and stakeholders in learning and achieving success together. **Developmental leaders** using emerging leadership concepts step back, creating opportunities for individuals to embark on their leadership journey. Both types of leadership emphasize empowering others and sharing roles and responsibilities. When combined into **Developmental Agile Leadership** and coupled with learning agility, trust, and hope to build resilience and a growth mindset, team members emerge as leaders who want to work on skilled teams with committed and effective teams and stakeholders. Nurturing current and future leaders establishes a legacy of growth that continues to inspire and develop others, and **shared leadership** promotes collective responsibility. Develop your leadership and empower others by applying the concepts in this book.

This book guides project leaders (sponsors, Product Owners, Scrum Masters, and project managers) in developing their teams and stakeholders. This book is also for:

- team members who want to lead, or at least significantly influence, parts of projects aligned with their expertise;
- stakeholders who want project teams to develop ever more useful solutions collaboratively;
- consultants, trainers, and educators seeking a leadership system based on learning goals, academic content, practical guidance, and bullet lists at the end of each major section in each chapter.

Contents

List of Figures and Tables

Figures

Tables

Three Guiding Ideas Behind Developmental Agile Leadership

This book uses three guiding ideas that are woven throughout every chapter. These ideas reflect a practical, human-centered approach to leadership in complex, changing environments.

1. **Embrace change by leading with learning agility, trust, hope, and a growth mindset:** Developmental Agile Leaders build environments where trust takes root, teams adapt together, and learning drives progress—even when the path ahead is uncertain.
2. **Empower others to lead by stepping back and leading from behind:** Instead of leading from the front, developmental leaders accompany others from behind—creating space for team members and stakeholders to step forward and grow into leadership.
3. **Anchor leadership in shared values, virtues, and stakeholder-centered purpose:** By combining Agile practices with servant and developmental leadership, Developmental Agile Leaders cultivate learning cultures grounded in shared purpose, real-time feedback, and deep respect for people.

Why This Book Stands Out

This book integrates Agile, servant, and developmental leadership into a stakeholder-centered model that equips leaders to trust, adapt, and grow alongside their teams, building leadership capacity in others, not just themselves.

Preface

Early in our careers, we worked as hands-on team members and project managers in various consulting roles and, later, as project management and leadership professors. We each published with many coauthors; however, this is our first collaboration.

We used an Agile approach to write this book. From the outset, our goal was to foster **individual leadership** and enhance collaboration among teams and stakeholders. Few publications cover both individual and team development. This collaboration is vital during periods of uncertainty. We use the acronym VUCA to capture the challenges of our rapidly changing times and how leaders can guide their teams through them.

Another key point we started with was that **people must trust their leaders**, or little else matters. Once we explored that further, we realized hope and learning agility work together with trust to create an effective culture. We also started by believing leaders must know and **actively embrace empowering principles and values**. Chapter 3 details **Agile leadership principles**, and Chapter 4 details **developmental leadership values**. Virtues and **values** work together to shape Developmental Agile Leadership. **Virtues** are inner strengths—like humility, courage, or integrity—that prepare us to act wisely, especially under pressure. They are enablers. **Values** are our guiding beliefs—like respect, collaboration, or personal growth—that point us in a desired direction. They are navigators. Effective leadership needs the vision of a compass and the energy of a battery.

Armed with an understanding and firm belief in both principles, the second half of this book describes how to implement them. Chapter 5 describes how teams and stakeholders learn, and Chapter 6 discusses how they achieve success together. Chapter 7 focuses on developing future leaders, and Chapter 8 ties the book together.

Each chapter highlights at least three key learning goals to guide readers. The book divides each chapter into three to six sections; each section ends with a bulleted list summarizing key leadership points.

We hope you enjoy and benefit from this book as much as we did in writing it.

Testimonials

"This brief book presents a systematic conceptual framework for understanding Developmental Agile Leadership. *It details insights and methods as a roadmap for Product Owners, project managers (Scrum Masters), team members, and stakeholders to develop inspiring and efficiently run teams. The book takes a gentle dive into all members' emotional, motivational, and growth issues."*—**David T. Hellkamp, PhD, Emeritus Professor of Clinical and Consulting Psychology**

*"*Developmental Agile Leadership *provides business leaders and future leaders with an invaluable guide and system. To effectively lead in the dynamic business environment, leaders must embrace VUCA challenges as great opportunities for growth and innovation. Further, the emphasis placed by Tim and Kam on the importance of the customer's involvement in the process is highly significant. Customers often anticipate or initiate situational changes and disruptions well before commercial market participants do."*—**Chris Tetrault, President—Tatro Inc. and Inventor of T COOL**

"The leadership advice in Chapter 2 of this exciting book can be truly transformative for personal and team effectiveness! It offers a refreshing view, emphasizing the importance of leaders being open and honest while embodying a growth mindset. It reinforced my belief that trust is the glue of life—by building trust, we empower others to grow, adapt, and lead confidently, even in uncertain times."—**Ashima Sharma, Founding Partner, Ayuka Consulting**

"In a VUCA world, leading differently is essential. Developmental Agile Leadership, *as described, is fresh and inviting, laying the foundation for adopting an Agile mindset and explaining its necessity. The tools and techniques discussed enable rapid acceleration into this new leadership style, allowing leaders to influence their teams effectively. The leader can then impart these skills to their team and stakeholders."*—**Frank M. Forte, Executive Leadership Coach, Author of** *A.G.I.L.E. Thinking Demystified*

"As an engineering manager at a dynamic startup, the insights from this book have been invaluable. Implementing the strategies for building trust and fostering a growth mindset has empowered my team to confidently navigate frequent changes. The practical strategies have helped us collaborate more effectively and adapt swiftly, significantly improving our product development process and team cohesion."—**Nick Kloppenborg, MS, PE, Senior Manager, Product Development**

"Leadership in action means facing challenges head-on with clarity and confidence. In times of uncertainty, rely on these proven, practical techniques that deliver results. Decision making does not need to be complicated. Empower your team, solve problems together, build trust, and drive success. What strategies are you using to tackle problems head-on and foster team development?"—**Connie Plowman, PMI Eric Jenett Project Management Excellence Award Recipient and Coauthor of *Developing Strengths-Based Project Teams* and *Project Communications***

"In our current economy, the concept of scaling or scalability drives a lot of the value of organizations. Creating environments that increase the likelihood of emergent leaders is the human capital development equivalent of scalability. In an environment where leaders are scarce, the ability to grow the next generation of leaders is a true competitive edge."—**Jesse Maleszewski, President, Sand Hill, Inc.**

"Given our work—leading complex commercial construction projects—we expect employees to step into leadership roles from day one. This book provides practical steps for coaching future leaders, emphasizing key learning opportunities, and adapting leadership styles to individual needs, fostering an environment where leadership development is expected."—**Cara Cross, SHRM-CP, Talent Services Vice President, Messer Construction Co.**

"I love this book! It offers a fresh perspective on leadership, integrating Agile and developmental leadership to empower individuals and teams. It challenges readers to reflect and adapt and cultivate trust, resilience, and learning agility. I love seeing stakeholder engagement take center stage, reinforcing leadership as a truly collaborative and dynamic process."—**Louise M. Worsley, Author of *Stakeholder-Led Project Management*, Visiting Lecturer, University of Cape Town, PMO Global Awards Judge**

PART 1

Embrace Developmental Agile Leadership Principles and Values

CHAPTER 1

Developmental Agile Leadership: The Challenges and Opportunities of an Uncertain World

The leader's job is not to have all the answers but to create an environment where others can find them.

—Senge (1990, 340)

Developmental Agile Leadership is a fulfilling journey of personal growth and effectiveness, empowering individuals, teams, and stakeholders to lead, especially during turbulent times. By cultivating your leadership skills and strengths and sharing leadership, you enable others to step into their leadership potential. Figure 1.1 shows that developmental and Agile leadership overlap, but each contributes to how leaders can be effective in a turbulent VUCA (volatility, uncertainty, complexity, and ambiguity) environment. The emphasis of developmental leadership is helping *individuals* grow and develop, while the emphasis for Agile leadership is helping *teams and stakeholders* grow and develop. With this approach, developmental leaders lead from behind, whether leading individuals or a team.

Learning Goals

- **Describe** how developmental and Agile leadership principles help leaders navigate uncertainty and build trust with stakeholders.
- **Describe** how seeking and openly receiving customer feedback helps teams learn rapidly and build trust.
- **Differentiate** between transformational, servant, and developmental leadership.

Chapter 1: VUCA Environment

Developmental Leadership

Agile Leadership

Learning Agility, Trust, and Hope

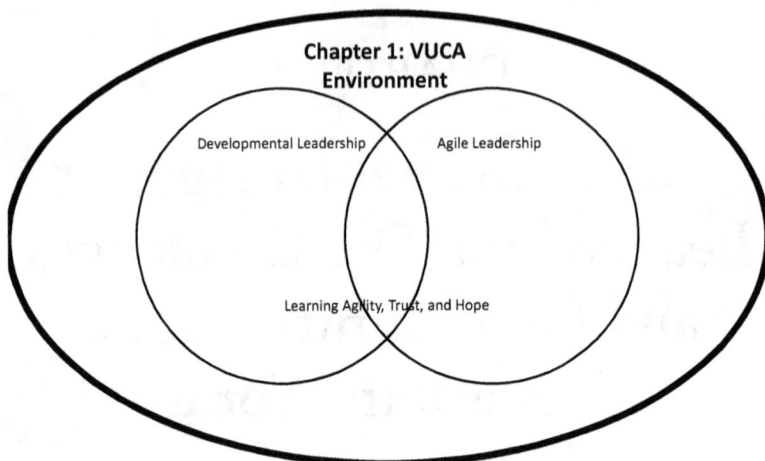

Figure 1.1 *Developmental Agile Leadership roadmap*

Introduction

We wrote this book in the ever-changing twenty-first century, aware that challenges and difficulties are unavoidable. Simple solutions are seldom sufficient, and uncertainty is a constant. This book helps you develop Agile leadership skills and guides your team through challenges. It also helps you understand and apply management strategies for today's challenges. This book draws from Agile principles, in which teams learn to "be agile," meaning they embody agility. Like Agile teams, this book uses an iterative process to help you develop skills. **Our primary aim is to help you develop as a leader and help you develop future leaders.**

You are not alone in this journey, and we are here to guide and support you. Our book has two halves: the first half covers leadership principles and values, and the second half presents Developmental Agile Leadership practices.

This book explores three elements of Developmental Agile Leadership:

1. **Principles**: Create a stakeholder-centered culture emphasizing learning agility, trust, and hope.
2. **Mindset**: Foster continuous learning through reflection and feedback.

3. **Developmental Agile Leadership**: Apply these principles and mindset to empower individuals, cultivate leadership, and strengthen teams.

Lead with values, think and act with agility, and prioritize collaboration.

Leadership is about helping others grow—when you share, support, and adapt, you build stronger teams and future leaders.

As you explore these principles and mindset, it's helpful to distinguish between values and virtues. Values act like a North Star; they guide direction and define what matters most to us as leaders. Virtues are like batteries; they reflect our inner character and readiness to act with integrity, courage, and humility. Values show where we're going; virtues help us get there. Both are essential for Developmental Agile Leadership, especially when leading with trust in uncertain environments.

We wrote our book with several hopes in mind.

- Through learning agility, trust, and hope, may this book guide your leadership and empower you and others.
- May collaborations allow you to build better workplaces that value every person's contribution.

By cultivating current and future leaders, we leave a legacy of continued growth and inspiration for others. Everyone is responsible for shared leadership.

This chapter examines concepts relevant to turbulent times and leadership styles to achieve better outcomes and growth.

Understand the VUCA Landscape

VUCA is an acronym for volatility, uncertainty, complexity, and ambiguity. It describes the ever-changing world, where constant change, disruption, and unpredictability are the norm. The acronym has its roots in the American military and was used to describe the world after the Cold War.

The concept was used to train and prepare army officers for the twenty-first century.

Shifting demographics, economies, politics, environments, societies, and technologies shape challenges in an uncertain world. Firms constantly strive to adapt, improve their strengths, reduce weaknesses, and identify opportunities and threats to compete. However, organizational success involves more than profit maximization. Successful **learning organizations** prioritize building a culture of care, support, and growth for employees and stakeholders. In learning organizations, employees show purpose and commitment across the organization.

A changing environment demands that traditional leadership styles evolve to ensure everyone flourishes. Personal and team development and stakeholder engagement are essential for leaders at all levels to respond swiftly and adapt to change. In doing so, teams develop collective competencies and strengths. In an unpredictable environment, developmental and Agile principles are crucial.

VUCA's challenges also present opportunities for leadership. We encourage you to see the potential for growth and innovation within this dynamic environment. We found the ideas by Bennett and Lemoine (2014) appealing because they broke down each element of VUCA:

- In **volatile** situations, change is frequent, and things are unstable, but pertinent information is available. One effective response is to make an **Agile** decision that could be modified quickly based upon subsequent changes. For example, when choosing between risky and safer stocks, market data helps you decide quickly.
- In **uncertain** situations, you may understand the causes and effects, not the outcome. A situation like this may warrant an **information-based** approach. For example, as cybersecurity threats become more menacing and frequent, you understand these threats can have severe business impacts on finances and confidential data. You may choose to strengthen encryption and software systems or focus on encryption.
- **Complexity** characterizes other situations where there are many moving parts, and there may be a significant interdependence between various factors, such as multiple stakeholders with different

priorities. When dealing with that type of complexity, we need to first uncover those priorities and then decide which we are going to satisfy or at least satisfy first and how we will explain our decisions and work with stakeholders whose priorities we cannot fully satisfy.

- **Ambiguity** may characterize some situations where precedence is lacking, so **experimentation** may help. For example, if you want to buy a new car, you might test-drive a hybrid or electric vehicle.

However, many challenging circumstances involve evolving combinations of volatility, uncertainty, complexity, and ambiguity. Shared leadership is key to effective management in challenging times such as these. **Through Developmental Agile Leadership, we believe cultivating your leadership skills and sharing leadership enables others to develop their leadership potential so that collectively we can meet these various and changing challenges.**

How Can Leaders Navigate the VUCA Environment?

Agile and developmental leadership practices are key in today's unpredictable world. These behaviors are based on concepts from Agile approaches to projects and developmental leadership from human resources management. The concepts involve leaders prioritizing customers and addressing their needs. We characterize developmental leadership as a form of informal leadership.

Prioritize Value from the Customer's Viewpoint

Agile leaders prioritize customer needs and expectations and focus on value by understanding what this means to customers. Agile leaders and teams prize delivering work products that satisfy customers.

Respond Quickly to Feedback and Continue to Learn

As rapid feedback drives improvements, leaders who build trust seek prompt, candid input from team members. Teams build trust with stakeholders and customers when they share work progress, partially developed concepts, and complete work products with them. These teams receive quick and helpful feedback to work on the next deliverable. This practice also shows that the team values stakeholders and incorporates their input.

Empower Individuals, Teams, and Stakeholders

Developmental leaders focus on shared goals and use trust-based partnerships to foster team growth (Gilley et al. 2011). Effective twenty-first-century leaders understand their dependence on others. We encourage you to create a **bias for action** with and through others to make progress so that all team members are self-assured in their decisions to enable progress; increased autonomy enhances project commitment.

Adapt to Changing Team Dynamics and Stakeholder Expectations

Many people experience feelings of isolation and want to belong to groups where they feel comfortable. The pandemic heightened these feelings, and online rather than in-person interactions can reinforce isolation. As workers have different preferences for autonomy and independence (and telling someone what to do rarely works well), leaders must understand individual motivations. This allows them to create meaningful work groups of team members and stakeholders.

Lead with Virtues to Navigate Unpredictable Challenges

Since leaders can adopt various approaches to address VUCA challenges, here are some **virtues** that can help. Remember that when situations involve **volatility**, where change is frequent, and things are unstable, leaders make quick decisions with *confidence* and *faith* in themselves and others; they do not let doubts hold them back. They *detach* from the issue so that they are free to choose how to act. They use *flexibility*, meaning that they consider others' ideas and feelings to rethink existing practices and solutions and consider new ones.

When situations involve **uncertainty**, leaders understand at least part of a problem, but not the solution. So, they gather data and consider the pros and cons, act with *trustworthiness,* and do their best. Leaders also show *self-discipline*, meaning they do not react but think things through before they act. Finally, leaders show *consideration for others* because they think about how their actions will affect them.

When circumstances involve **complexity**, there are many moving parts, and it is hard to keep things straight. Leaders need to reorganize and reframe their thinking with *purpose*. In these situations, they begin with a vision and focus on the goals. They do one thing at a time. Complex situations warrant *creativity,* so leaders consider the issue from different perspectives. These situations also require cooperation, so working together both as a team and with stakeholders is important.

When a situation involves **ambiguity**, uncertainty reigns. Because leaders can expect the unexpected, they need to experiment and even pivot based on the results. They pivot with *perseverance,* which helps them overcome obstacles, pace themselves, and remain steadfast with the team. *These circumstances also warrant forgiveness*, whereby they give themselves and others another chance. They own their mistakes, and they are understanding. Last, these situations require *responsibility,* meaning that leaders accept accountability for their actions, and when they make a mistake, they make amends and do not make excuses.

With all that leaders do to navigate the VUCA environment, they also develop **self-awareness** of their strengths and biases. This helps them understand their behaviors so that they are better positioned to empower others and helps them lead. Effective leaders have a clear vision, interpersonal abilities, and adaptability. These qualities are a starting point for developing confident and ethical leadership. As you build your skills and strengths to lead, you become more effective in helping others do the same through Developmental Agile Leadership.

We encourage you to:

- **put customers first** and work together to meet their needs and define success from their perspective;
- **respond quickly to feedback** and continue to build trust, remain open to input, and incorporate it to improve customer value;
- **empower others** and help them make decisions so that they too can contribute to a culture of trust; and
- **remain adaptive** and adjust how you lead to changing individual and team needs.

Agile leaders create trusting, adaptable, collaborative teams that handle uncertainty well.

Leadership Approaches for a Changing World

New leadership styles are essential in the VUCA world. For the best results, we encourage you to try different leadership styles, such as Agile, transformational, servant, and developmental. Our book emphasizes developmental and Agile leadership. We begin with Agile leadership.

Agile Leadership Guides from the Front, Middle, and Behind

Agile leadership is essential in a VUCA environment. Agile leaders adjust their leadership styles, incorporating transformational, servant, and developmental approaches. To understand Agile leadership, consider leadership in terms of Agile project management. In Agile software development, project managers lead teams through sprints. Sprinting involves running for a short period, as quickly as possible, with as much effort as possible. Similarly, Agile teams complete short work cycles, known as sprints. Agile leaders empower teams and promote a learning environment for them to experiment, innovate, and improve. These quick adaptations to change and not fearing failure are hallmarks of Agile leaders and their teams (Bragger et al. 2021).

In an Agile environment, teams share leadership. For example, the Product Owner represents stakeholders and the Scrum Master (scrum lead or Agile coach) supports the team rather than directing them. Between them, they:

- start the project with a charter as an overarching guide so that all participants work toward the common goal;
- lead with principles and virtues, including trust and accountability;
- use open communication, collaborative decisions, and effective conflict resolution strategies to ensure team agreement and project success;
- provide resources, support, and collaborate with users and developers to meet stakeholder needs;

- plan, experiment, learn, and evaluate together; and
- focus on benefits and problem-solving for all stakeholders, not just meeting specifications.

Agile leaders encourage **learning and adaptation**, which are core tenets of developmental leadership. Agile leadership comprises sharing leadership and project roles.

Transformational Leadership Inspires Change from the Front

Transformational leaders inspire teams to pursue a greater purpose. These leaders lead from the front (and are typically senior executives); they challenge ideas, take risks, create a plan, and lead their team to make it happen. Transformational leadership begins with a clear vision and a path to reach it. Transformational leaders concentrate on immediate and long-range goals. They create and describe the vision and explain how each team member can contribute and benefit. Transformational leaders are optimistic about followers' ability to meet goals, enhancing team spirit. **Consider the transformational leadership approach for dramatic change initiatives.**

Servant Leadership Empowers from the Middle

A servant leader's primary goal is to help people do their work by prioritizing followers' needs and sharing power with them. Servant leaders lead from the middle and assist their teams in overcoming daily challenges. They are often called supportive and cooperative leaders. These leaders focus on the short term, helping people do their work. Servant leaders also help teams in crises. To servant leaders, their work is a calling.

Servant leaders put their followers first and anticipate and address their needs. They often confer with their teammates and help plan activities before, during, and after work to support everyone. An expression that describes how they support team members is that they "carry food and water." This metaphor suggests that these leaders prioritize service and support. They do whatever is necessary (big or small) to help their team succeed. **Consider servant leadership as centered on the team's needs.**

Developmental Leadership Cocreates Individual Leadership from Behind

> *A leader ... is like a shepherd. He stays behind the flock, letting the most nimble go out ahead, whereupon the others follow, not realizing that all along they are being directed from behind.*
>
> —Mandela (1994, 18)

Mandela's quote is impactful and reflects guiding team growth, not dictating it—that's developmental leadership (Hill 2010). Developmental leadership provides individuals with the tools they need to grow and flourish. This approach helps people become leaders who mentor others and improve projects or organizations. Another aspect of developmental leadership is that it builds **self-efficacy**. People with self-efficacy trust their abilities and are motivated to achieve goals.

Developmental leaders focus on people's long-term development and engage everyone in personal growth. Developmental leaders guide and influence others to lead by stepping back when appropriate and letting others lead. They encourage new ideas, experimentation, and member participation in a safe and supportive environment.

Developmental leadership emphasizes leveraging informal practices for individual growth and innovation. Consider the developmental leader within this context because the leader:

- focuses on each team member to help them develop and extend their knowledge, skills, and abilities;
- supports team members' growth through coaching, mentoring, and training; and
- models effective leadership behaviors.

This book emphasizes self-improvement and helping others as essential leadership skills. These changes result in improvements and transformations.

Blend Developmental and Agile Leadership Styles for Greater Impact

Developmental leadership helps individuals develop leadership skills in various situations. Developmental Agile Leaders enhance collaboration and achieve faster progress. Several essential virtues for Developmental Agile Leadership are **learning agility, trust,** and **hope**. Among these, learning agility involves adapting to new situations quickly, trust requires faith in others and hope is a positive mindset.

We encourage you to:

- **adapt your leadership style** to the team's needs and situation;
- **support your team's development** and help them grow and take on leadership tasks; and
- **encourage teamwork and trust** with open communication and shared decision making.

Leadership is a continuous journey of learning and improvement. Chapter 1 shows that developmental and Agile leadership help teams innovate and adapt. Leaders empower their teams and embrace customer feedback. Leaders also help their teams grow so everyone can take on leadership roles. **Agile and developmental leadership styles make strong, flexible teams that succeed in uncertain times.**

As you begin your Developmental Agile Leadership journey, note that we combine these concepts in this book. Developmental Agile Leaders offer a supportive, behind-the-scenes presence, and Agile methodologies involve shared leadership and work in dynamic environments with their teams.

Developmental leadership + Agile = Developmental Agile Leadership

---

Embrace the opportunity to put these principles into your leadership practice.

In a world of uncertainty, your ability to lead with agility, trust, and purpose will define your impact—step forward with confidence and shape the future, one decision at a time.

The next chapter focuses on learning agility, trust, and hope. These elements are key drivers of team member and stakeholder motivation and inspiration.

An Overview of How This Book Can Help You Lead

This book shows leaders how to use leadership skills to help their teams thrive in uncertain times. The first half covers leadership concepts, laying the foundation for leadership practices and the second half focuses on practical applications, explaining why these ideas are essential.

Part 1: Embrace Developmental Agile Leadership Principles and Values

Chapter 1 introduces VUCA concepts and transformational, servant, developmental, and Agile leadership styles.

Chapter 2 describes learning agility, trust, hope, and a growth mindset. Developmental leaders are learning agile. Leaders who learn to adapt and cultivate trust and hope foster thriving, resilient workplaces.

Chapter 3 covers core Agile principles, related roles and communication strategies, and leadership styles. We commonly characterize servant leadership as "agile." Self-managed Agile teams create innovative solutions by focusing on customer value and continuous improvement.

Chapter 4 focuses on developmental leadership. As leaders engage in developmental leadership, they lead from behind and align values with actions. In doing so, they help others grow into emergent leaders.

Part 2: Implement Developmental Agile Leadership Practices

Chapter 5 applies concepts from previous chapters and explains how to build a culture that inspires teams to learn and lead together. The chapter focuses on trust, hope, and continuous improvement.

Chapter 6 offers practical suggestions for team and stakeholder engagement. The process includes improving team meetings, decisions, conflict resolution, and stakeholder relationships.

Chapter 7 describes how leaders cultivate emergent leadership and develop the leaders of tomorrow. The goal is to build a leadership culture of shared growth and empowerment.

Chapter 8 concludes by bringing it all together with our hope that this book empowers you to navigate a complex world with resilience. We hope you use the ideas in this book to enhance your leadership and help others reach their potential.

We encourage you to trust your judgment and build upon the insights from this book to guide you on your journey.

What Sets This Book Apart?

This book offers a distinctive approach to leadership because we:

- focus on Developmental Agile Leadership, which involves informal leadership to support others from behind to help them grow. We combine developmental leadership and Agile concepts to explore elements of Developmental Agile Leadership (principles and mindset).
- anchor it in virtues (learning agility, trust, and hope).
- support adopting a growth mindset for continuous learning and adaptation.
- anchor it in the concept of care in management (von Krogh 1998). Self-care and confidence in ourselves help us develop care for others. High-care environments support knowledge sharing, creativity, and innovation.

Ways to Engage with This Book

Readers have different interests and learning styles influencing how they engage with a book. Whereas many read a book from cover to cover, others may be interested in certain topics or chapters. Some readers may want to read and use this book as a personal development workbook. Chapter 7, for example, covers practices for cultivating emergent leadership in others. From our experiences, journaling and reflective learning are excellent ways to develop oneself and work with others to share insights.

We begin each chapter with learning goals and conclude with a section on reflective experiential learning questions. For those readers interested in specific themes, each chapter contains subheadings, and the index of the book is another way to identify topics of interest.

Learn, Reflect, and Grow

Everyone has a unique way of learning and identifying areas for growth. Visual learners may want to express their ideas with images or mind maps using colors. Auditory learners may prefer to keep an audio journal, learn from podcasts, or express their ideas through storytelling. Learners may prefer to read and write their ideas and keep lists or use a logical problem-solving approach based on data to track progress. Others may prefer to interact in groups to exchange ideas and feedback. Introspective learners may thrive by learning and reflecting on their own. Think about different learning styles when you journal to understand better and remember things.

Improving skills is easier through experiential learning—"knowing, doing, and reflecting" (Kolb 2014). Reflection through journaling helps develop leadership and courage. Review the following format for ideas on journal topics as you go through the chapters:

- **What do I know?** Ask this question to identify current skills, experiences, and insights.
- **What am I doing?** Ask this question to journal about current actions and behaviors and what you can do to improve your leadership growth.
- **What am I reflecting on?** This question can prompt reflections on challenges, lessons learned, and new insights.

The experiential learning process is also about team growth and development (Kolb 2014). Adapt the above questions to help teams with group growth and development by asking:

- **What do we know?**
- **What are we doing?**
- **What are we reflecting on?**

Figure 1.2 illustrates the connections between these questions.

First, the connection between "What do I know?" and "What am I doing?" involves growth in knowledge and action. Then, the connection between "What am I doing?" and "What am I reflecting on?" involves growth between action and reflection. Then, notice how repeating the steps in the process enables further growth and development. You can also start the cycle in any of the three steps.

This cycle is about improvement and change. It is a cycle of personal and team growth and development. Cultivating current and future leaders leaves a legacy of growth that continues to inspire and develop others. **Shared leadership is a collective responsibility.**

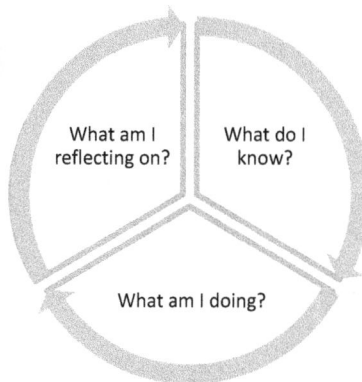

Figure 1.2 The experiential learning process (Kolb 2014)

CHAPTER 2

Build a Strong Foundation: Cultivate Learning Agility, Trust, and Hope

Trust is the glue of life. It's the most essential ingredient in effective communication. It's the foundational principle that holds all relationships.

—Covey (1995, 203)

Figure 2.1 demonstrates that learning agility, trust, and hope are essential for leaders in a VUCA environment.

Learning Goals

- **Explain** how learning agility, trust, and hope enhance team resilience and performance.
- **Describe** the impact of psychological safety on team motivation and adaptability.
- **Apply** learning agility, trust, and hope to address a leadership challenge and improve team outcomes.

Introduction

Chapter 1 covers the challenges of a changing world and different leadership approaches. Developmental and Agile leadership is a successful combination because strong leadership, clear goals, and a learning culture drive high-performing companies.

This chapter focuses on learning agility, trust, and hope. These three principles are key for leaders creating a vibrant workplace. How do

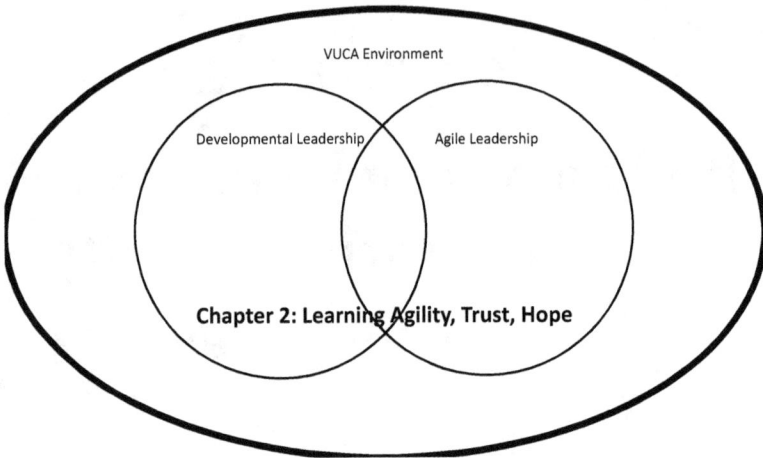

Figure 2.1 Developmental Agile Leadership roadmap

leaders cultivate this ideal workplace? To answer this, we look at the key traits of developmental and Agile leaders and some leadership foundations from positive psychology. People develop learning agility through experience and adaptability. This mindset, when embraced by leaders, improves team adaptability. Trust requires openness to others and an optimistic view of their actions. Because it is a positive state of mind, hope helps us set realistic goals with purpose and perseverance. Imagine a dysfunctional workplace lacking trust, hope, and learning agility. **A strong, dynamic workplace that embodies these principles is well worth fostering.**

These three elements—learning agility, trust, and hope—function as values and virtues. As values, they signal what matters in the culture we strive to build. Leaders and teams embody virtues and bring them to life through action and character. This dual role makes them especially powerful in shaping resilient, developmental teams.

Nurture Learning Agility for Continuous Growth

The whole is greater than the sum of its parts.
—Aristotle (1984, 1045a. 8–10)

Researchers describe learning agility as learning from previous experiences to adapt to new situations (De Meuse et al. 2008). **Learning**

has to do with expanding your knowledge base. We learn by using different learning styles that are based on our senses. Skill development occurs through doing, seeing, hearing, and sharing ideas. As we learn, we advance technical and interpersonal skills and sharpen our minds. We also learn to adapt behaviors through curiosity and openness to new perspectives. **Agility** suggests physical and mental strength, balance, coordination, and speed.

When combined, the literature refers to learning agility as a **leadership meta-competency**. Another word for meta-competency is core competence or a superpower. "You recognize it upon seeing it" is a fitting way to describe someone with learning potential. Does someone come to mind when you visualize someone with a meta-competency, like learning agility?

Many describe learning agility as a **growth mindset** characterized by continuous learning and adaptation. We develop skills and abilities by acquiring, transferring, and using knowledge and capabilities to learn through practice. Our mindset shapes our skills and abilities, and mindsets reflect adaptive or maladaptive motivational patterns.

People with a growth mindset believe their abilities can develop, unlike those with a fixed mindset (Dweck 1986). A fixed mindset is fear-based and leads to avoiding challenges. In contrast, those with a growth mindset understand that abilities develop through trying, learning, and persisting. A growth mindset reflects resilience and a desire to grow. Dweck's concepts apply to individual, team, and organizational leadership (Table 2.1).

Table 2.1 Fixed versus growth mindset

When I face	With a fixed mindset, I tend to	With a growth mindset, I tend to
Challenges	Avoid challenges	Embrace challenges
Obstacles	Be defensive	Persist
Effort	Give up and not try	Persist to succeed
Criticism	Ignore it	Learn from it
Others succeeding	Experience a sense of threat	Get inspired and learn
Outcomes	Underachieve full potential	Achieve full potential

Adapted from Dweck (2009).

Even when difficult, embracing others' perspectives helps us grow and learn from experiences. This shows that leadership is reciprocal, and that there is a shared responsibility within and between teams. Individuals with adaptive agility readily leave their comfort zone and try something new. They will take risks, fail, and be OK with failing because they try again … and again. This reflects persistence and resilience. Everyone can develop a growth mindset for learning agility.

Develop a Growth Mindset for Learning Agility

Individuals with learning agility have:

- *mental agility* and are quick and flexible problem solvers;
- *people agility* and communicate effectively; they collaborate with others, and as they help others, they develop themselves;
- *change agility* and manage change with an open mind; they enjoy experimenting and show no fear;
- *results agility* and produce results when faced with new situations; and
- *self-awareness* and are open-minded and adaptive in their thinking and behaviors as they learn from experiences.

Learning-agile individuals succeed in different roles and attain career success (De Meuse et al. 2008). The literature defines them as having "**high leadership potential**" (Church and Seaton 2022) and suggests that anyone can develop learning dexterity and assist others in becoming better leaders. Envision working for someone with high adaptive capacity and how much you could learn. Visualize being mentored by someone with an adaptable skill set and imagine team achievements within a learning-agile system. **That is the power of learning agility.**

For knowledge work to flourish, the workplace must be one where people feel able to share their knowledge! This means sharing concerns, questions, mistakes, and half-formed ideas.

—Edmondson (2019, 123)

Encourage Teams to Embrace Change and Learning

Strong leaders build resilient and innovative teams when they:

- coach and mentor others;
- promote experimentation;
- provide learning opportunities;
- create a workplace where:
  - a culture of psychological safety and a growth mindset allows for risk-taking, open communication, and learning from mistakes;
  - mistakes are encouraged so that everyone learns from them. There is a culture of learning to fail to make progress (Edmondson 2023);
- encourage networking to enhance collaboration and improve growth and development (De Meuse 2017).

Finding out that you are wrong is even more valuable than being right, because you are learning.

—Edmondson (2019, 45)

Organizations that learn have a competitive advantage because they are nimble and innovative; they adapt to change and inspire individuals and stakeholders. **This is a learning culture.**

Connect Learning Agility with Developmental Leadership

To connect learning agility to developmental leadership, recall that developmental leadership involves informally leading from behind. This leadership approach emphasizes continuous learning, a supportive culture, and shared workloads to foster growth. Developmental leaders are learning agile.

Those who develop learning agility as a meta-competency—whether as a superpower or core strength—are high achievers who help bring out the best in us. They encourage us to learn from mistakes because the more we do that, the more we can help others do the same, and create a workplace where everyone succeeds. When there is genuine trust and hope in the workplace, people form healthy collaborations and sustain trust and hope. This type of organization is innovative and creative. It values employee well-being and engagement beyond financial metrics. **A trusting culture of shared leadership helps organizations succeed.**

We encourage you to:

- **step into new and uncomfortable situations** by taking on a challenge that pushes your abilities; then reflect on what you learned;
- **reframe failure as a learning opportunity** by focusing on what you learned and not dwelling on mistakes
- **have open discussions** about growth; and
- **create a safe space** for others to share ideas and take risks.

Growth in learning agility is one facet of effective leadership, as team success also hinges on trust among members and their leaders.

Foster a Culture of Trust

Trust means being open and vulnerable to others and believing in their good intentions (Norman et al. 2010). Trust is essential in the VUCA world because it builds strong working relationships. Without trust, collaboration and innovation suffer. Trustworthy leaders instill trust in their followers and inspire hope. Like project managers, effective leaders combine technical skills and strong interpersonal abilities.

You may have heard of the "trust falls" exercise, a team-building exercise where one person stands in front of another person and falls backward. The person falling backward trusts their partner to catch them. Visualize yourself and a trusted person performing this exercise. You trust this person who delivers on their promises because this person is dependable, supportive, and caring. Now, imagine doing the exercise with someone you do not trust. Who is your preferred colleague or manager? Also, notice how trust is abstract, elusive, and powerful. Yet, trust is also fragile because rebuilding trust after it breaks is difficult. **Trust is so visceral that you sense it when it is there and when it is not.**

Key Traits of a Trustworthy Leader

You understand that trust is present as you perceive and experience it. You can tell that trust is lacking when your "Spidey senses tingle." Or you have an experience that breaks the trust or confirms your suspicions that someone is untrustworthy. You also sense (or suspect) that something is off about someone, so your interactions with this individual may be cautious. Trust is based on our emotions and rationality (or hearts and minds). Emotional trust develops from feelings, shared interests, and values (Bligh 2017) and is used to build positive social relationships; rational or cognitive trust (2017) is based on logic and information. Those who meet the emotional and rational dimensions of trust are authentic. Authentic leaders are optimistic and communicate with transparency (openness and honesty).

Another way of thinking about trustworthy individuals is that they walk the talk. People with trustworthy qualities exhibit many virtues and behaviors (Burke et al. 2007; Dirks and Skarlicki 2007; Hassan and Ahmed 2011; Bligh 2017) (Table 2.2).

Tim has two rules for estimating, whether estimating time, cost, or anything else. *Rule number one is don't lie to yourself, and rule number two is don't lie to others.* We love our projects and often have grand passion and enthusiasm for them. We can get so caught up in the potential of our ideas that we overlook the difficulties inherent in building a great solution for the stakeholder. When that happens, we sometimes lie to ourselves about the probability that we will be successful. Most of our projects compete to be selected. We often bid against competitors or negotiate with customers for external projects. For projects internal to our organization, we compete with other projects and ongoing work for resources. We might over promise in both cases, suggesting we can exceed expectations by doing more, finishing faster, and at a lower cost. When we are

Table 2.2 **Qualities of trustworthiness**

Inspires confidence by being	Encourages participation by being	Drives decision making by being	Enhances optimism by being	Spurs innovation by being
Open and honest (transparent)	Fair	A team builder	Motivational	Flexible
Predictable and dependable	Ethical	Consultative	Inspiring	Intuitive
Credible	Benevolent	A shared decision maker	Constructive	Effective at managing ambiguity
Authentic (natural)	Supportive and inclusive	A coach	Flexible	Creative
Competent	Empathetic	An effective influencer	Positive	

honest with ourselves and others, it fosters trust and realistic expectations of project completion.

Thinking about people you trust involves considering their strengths and virtues. We share common visions and values with those we trust (Palanski and Yammarino 2009). Integrity is also essential for trust; individuals with integrity keep their promises and follow through. Other virtues of trust include authenticity, courage, honesty, and fairness.

Developmental leadership shares many characteristics with servant leadership (Greenleaf 1998). Servant leaders are of service to others, so much so that they practice as if it were a calling. Key traits of servant leaders include altruism, vision, trust, empowerment, love, humility, and service (Winston and Patterson 2003). Some see environmental awareness and foresight as aspects of servant leadership (Searle and Barbuto Jr 2011). Coaching involves offering constructive feedback and helping set goals, and these practices align with servant leadership (Ely et al. 2010). Cerff and Winston (2006) suggest hope as another dimension of servant leadership. Servant leaders reflect humility and kindness and empower and inspire others to reach their full potential. Trust fosters hope and shared leadership.

How Trust Drives Team Success

One of the best ways to develop trust is to show this through actions, words, and behaviors. When leaders are genuine, employees experience optimism and collaborate effectively. True leaders share their power. In doing so, teams leverage their individual and collective expertise, experience, and abilities. Genuine experiences motivate team members to achieve common goals.

We experience more involvement when we work for a genuine leader because an authentic leader fosters interpersonal trust (Hassan and Ahmed 2011). Trust is reciprocal and, just as leaders foster confidence and optimism within teams, team members develop trust in each other and their leaders. Trust between group members helps buffer tasks and relationship conflicts. Although it is hard work to maintain trust in multiple relationships, it is not impossible, and it is vital to leading in a VUCA environment. When there is interpersonal trust, we depend on leaders to support and care for us, and we care for each other.

Authentic leadership promotes self-development (Rego et al. 2014). When we are our best selves at work, we are more productive, happier, and have a genuine sense of purpose for work. Trust builds better teamwork because everyone knows what to expect, and is more willing to work together and take risks. Trust is a buffer against negative work experiences like stress and burnout. When we hesitate to trust, it contributes to task cautiousness, which affects confidence and job performance. Over time, this may lead to mistrust, discouragement, and hopelessness. Building and maintaining trust is essential and inspirational.

We encourage you to:

- **be consistent**, keep your promises, and act with integrity to build trust;
- **create a safe and open environment** where people are comfortable sharing ideas and taking risks; and
- **empower others** through teamwork and shared leadership by valuing their contributions.

Trust Lays the Foundation for Collaboration and Innovation

Instill Hope to Build Resilience and Motivation

Hope is a positive motivational state (Snyder 2002). Like trust, hope involves rational thoughts and emotions. Hope helps us set realistic goals and act because we have agency and confidence (Reichard et al. 2013). Agency means we develop intentions and control actions and behaviors. A classic authority on hope research described hope as a rainbow:

> This reminds me of the rainbow that frequently is used as a symbol of hope. A rainbow is a prism that sends shards of multicolored light in various directions. It lifts our spirits and makes us think of what is possible. Hope is the same—a personal rainbow of the mind. (Snyder 2002, 269)

Snider's "personal rainbow of the mind" metaphor reflects vivid positivity and optimism. By fostering hope, leaders inspire perseverance and engagement. Like trust, hope is essential in an interdependent and uncertain world. Hope is more than an emotion; it is a powerful mental process (Helland and Winston 2005). Consider hope as a psychological resource (Hannah et al. 2009).

The Power of Collective Hope

Think of collective hope as WePower. Colla et al. (2022) show that while Snyder (2002) views hope at the individual level, it also applies to groups. Hope enhances pro-social behaviors, steps we take to help and benefit others. Hope, similar to trust, fosters collective well-being. Colla et al. used four intriguing terms to frame hope:

- **WillPower** is the personal motivation to be hopeful.
- **WayPower** is the personal plan to attain goals.
- **WhyPower** is the personal experience of hope.
- **WePower** is the interpersonal hope.

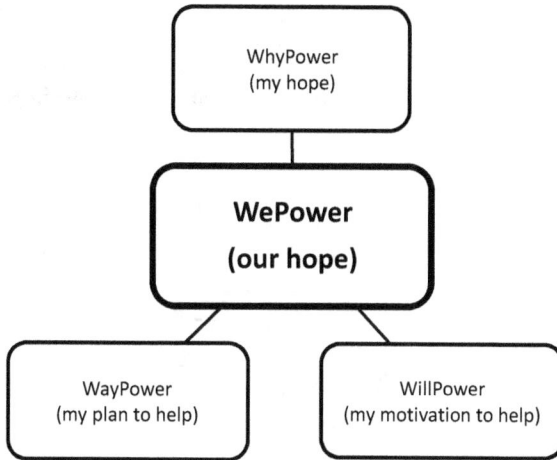

Figure 2.2 Collective hope is WePower (Colla et al. 2022)

Figure 2.2, as adapted from Colla et al. (2022) shows how WillPower, WayPower, WhyPower, and WePower represent strength and togetherness.

Many people seek meaningful work; a hopeful workplace enhances opportunities. Leaders instill hope to help followers reach their personal goals (Colla et al. 2022). When an organization has hope, it enhances retention, satisfaction, and commitment. Does this resemble your work, or is it in contrast to your workplace? What does that suggest about leadership, trust, and hope in your workplace?

Hope is a virtue, and as we express and show hopefulness, we motivate and benefit others. Hope is a positive organizational behavior (Youssef and Luthans 2007), and other forms of positive organizational behavior include resilience and optimism. These behaviors are psychological capabilities that help improve performance, job satisfaction, work happiness, and organizational commitment. Resilience is the capacity to bounce back from hardships and frustrations (Ledesma 2014), so resilient individuals are optimistic. **Remember, collective Hope is WePower (our hope).**

How Hope Shapes Team Performance and Engagement

Table 2.3 summarizes examples of outcomes of hope (Reichard et al. 2013).

Table 2.3 Hope and work outcomes

Positive work outcomes	Positive personal outcomes	Adverse outcomes when hope is missing
Job performance	Job satisfaction	Turnover
Financial performance	Organizational commitment	Absenteeism
Competitive advantage	Retention	Counterproductive behaviors
Training performance	Creativity	Stress
	Optimism	Burnout
	Well-being	Negative affect
	Emotional engagement	
	Meaning	
	Self-determination	
	Overall health	
	Gratitude	
	Happiness	
	Self-determination	
	Positive affect	

Adapted from Reichard et al. 2013.

Hopefulness is an ability we can all develop. Hope, like trust, is experienced and interpreted based on what someone says and does. As VUCA challenges warrant creativity and innovation, creativity is about having new ideas and innovation is using them to create products, services, processes, and procedures (Hughes et al. 2018). To nurture creative changes, it is important for the workplace to be optimistic.

We encourage you to:

- **foster optimism** by urging your team to trust in their capacity to reach objectives;
- **build collective hope and unity** by sharing goals and supporting each other; and
- **support resilience and optimism** by helping your team bounce back from setbacks and stay focused on solutions.

Cultivating trust, hope, and learning agility inspires everyone involved, and these principles foster Agile and developmental leadership approaches. The combinations enable organizations to thrive. **Growing and helping teams and stakeholders grow helps everyone succeed.**

Hope fuels motivation, trust strengthens relationships, and learning agility keeps teams adaptable. **Together, these qualities create a resilient and high-performing team.**

Integrate Learning Agility, Trust, and Hope for Team Success

Learning agility, trust, and hope drive motivation, leadership, and team effectiveness. Mastering agility requires openness to new experiences and learning from them. When combined, these qualities create the basis for high-performing teams. Adaptable leaders guide teams and stakeholders toward growth. We develop effective relationships and collaborate when we have faith in others through trust. Trust builds safe, respectful workplaces where everyone contributes and learns. When we are hopeful, we are optimistic about the future. Hope helps us visualize successes and work toward them. These three reinforcing principles are vital for leadership development and fundamental for resilient leadership and high-performing teams.

To conclude, Chapter 2 focuses on learning agility, trust, and hope to inspire teams and stakeholders. Learning agility involves quick adaptations, being receptive to change, and solving problems. Trust means honesty and building relationships where people are secure and collaborate. By setting realistic goals and being optimistic, hope helps motivate us and team members to be confident in what we do. **Leaders who are Agile learners build trust and inspire hope to create resilient, thriving workplaces.**

Embrace the opportunity to put these principles into your leadership practice.

Trust fuels collaboration, learning agility drives growth, and hope sustains momentum—embrace these foundations, and watch your leadership transform those around you.

The next chapter is on Agile leadership in action. The chapter covers core Agile principles, related roles and communication strategies, and leadership styles.

Learn, Reflect, and Grow

Everyone has a unique way of learning and identifying areas for growth. As outlined at the end of Chapter 1, we encourage you to keep a journal. Improving skills is easier through experiential learning—"knowing, doing, and reflecting" (Kolb 2014). Review the following formats for ideas on journal topics:

- **What do I know?**
- **What am I doing?**
- **What am I reflecting on?**
- **What do we know?**
- **What are we doing?**
- **What are we reflecting on?**

This cycle is about improvement and change. It is a cycle of personal and team growth and development. Cultivating current and future leaders leaves a legacy of growth that continues to inspire and develop others (Figure 2.3). **Shared leadership is a collective responsibility.**

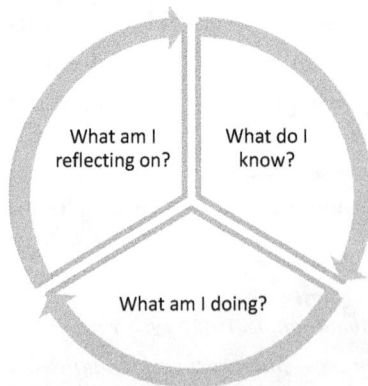

Figure 2.3 The experiential learning process (Kolb 2014)

CHAPTER 3

Agile Leadership in Action: Empower Teams to Adapt, Learn, and Succeed

Agile is an attitude, not a technique with boundaries. An attitude has no boundaries, so we wouldn't ask 'can I use agile here,' but rather 'how would I act in the agile way here?' or 'how agile can we be, here?'
—(Cockburn, n.d.)

Figure 3.1 shows that this chapter introduces Agile leadership concepts leaders can effectively use.

Learning Goals

- **Explain** the core principles of Agile leadership and their role in helping teams adapt, collaborate, and deliver value.
- **Apply** communication strategies that promote transparency, trust, and alignment in Agile teams.
- **Clarify** the roles of Agile leaders (Product Owners, Scrum Masters, and sponsors) in supporting team success.
- **Adapt** transformational, servant, and developmental leadership styles to empower self-managed teams.

Introduction

The previous chapter (**Chapter 2**) shows that **learning agility, trust, and hope are the basis of Agile leadership.** The chapter focuses on these concepts for shared decision making and teamwork.

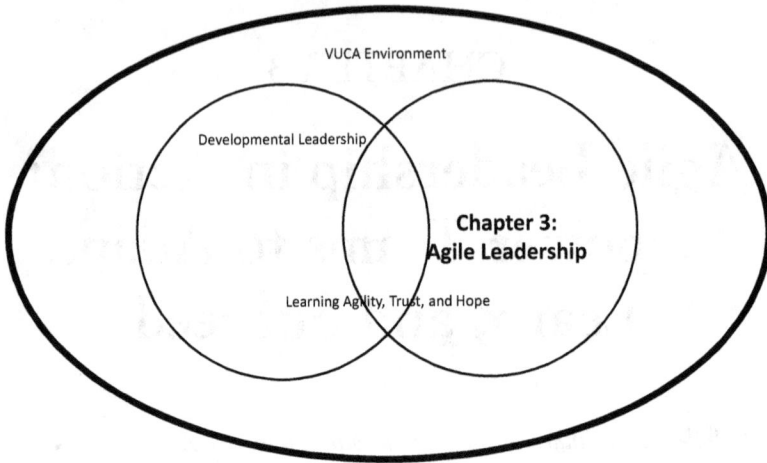

Figure 3.1 Developmental Agile Leadership roadmap

This chapter explores Agile leadership and how empowered teams adapt, learn, and succeed. The chapter examines the connections between Agile and leadership to help leaders build high-performing teams. **Agile leaders build trust, encourage innovation, and help their teams and customers succeed.**

What Is Agile Leadership, and Why Does It Matter?

Agile delivers valuable products to the customer through teamwork and open communication. Software developers and leaders follow the Agile Alliance values.

We are uncovering better ways of developing software by doing it and helping others do it. Through this work, we have come to value:

- **individuals and interactions** over processes and tools,
- **working software** over comprehensive documentation,
- **customer collaboration** over contract negotiation, and
- **responding to change** by following a plan.

That is, while there is value in the items on the right, we value the items on the left more (Beck et al. 2001).

Although the Manifesto creators call it "mushy stuff," the essence is to "act" in all ways that people are important, or "**be agile, do agile**" (Anantatmula and Kloppenborg 2021). Agile values active collaborations and flexibility, unlike traditional, plan-driven project management, that emphasize following a set plan, documentation, and process. According to Agile, customer feedback improves people, processes, and products, and this feedback loop fosters continuous learning and adaptation.

In a VUCA environment, many organizations use the Agile approach for projects.

- **Volatility** means things change frequently. Agile teams adapt to customer expectations and work quickly to deliver valuable work products. They strive to keep customers happy.
- **Uncertainty** suggests the need to gather more information before deciding. Agile teams work in short cycles and constantly seek stakeholder input to help them make sound decisions.
- **Complexity** sometimes means it is difficult to understand the entire situation. Agile teams focus on one or two work products at a time and adapt as needed.
- **Ambiguity** means that there is no precedence. Agile teams use creativity and experimentation.

Agile teams continually test and refine work products to meet evolving stakeholder needs.

Core Priorities for Agile Leaders

Agile's first and most important priority is satisfying customers, so the focus is on product value. Think about satisfying customers and keeping them happy as a **mindset** (attitude). The Agile system is dynamic, and work advances quickly. To succeed with Agile, leaders empower their teams to use rapid and honest communication as they develop solutions.

Deliver Value to Customers and Stakeholders

Agile emphasizes understanding and developing strong relationships with many stakeholders. Using a matrix to identify potential stakeholders, Agile leaders strive to identify, understand, prioritize, help, and learn from their stakeholders comprising individuals, groups, or organizations. The process also helps identify supportive stakeholders and those who may oppose the project. Once identified, the team strives to understand the needs and desires of each stakeholder so that they can manage expectations. One way they do this is to create **personas** (pretend users with some descriptive details) to guide their work. This process involves identifying individuals by name and characteristics to personify a customer regarding project deliverable functionality and its importance. This extensive wish list of stakeholder desires (a **backlog**) requires prioritization. The **Product Owner** plays an essential role in managing the backlog. Because the team now understands stakeholder goals, they help stakeholders reach them.

The core of Agile is a commitment to deliver value early and often because delivering and evaluating valuable features leads to project success. Agile teams typically focus on one or two key work products (or user stories/features) at a time, ensuring they deliver incremental value.

Customer satisfaction metrics (as determined by stakeholders) include viability, value, predictability, quality, and happiness. Delivering quality features builds stakeholder confidence, so predictability and quality are valuable metrics. Some projects provide value in larger increments rather than every week. In these cases, teams strive to help customers determine if the emerging work product is viable. Teams often inquire about stakeholders' satisfaction levels, to assess if they are pleased or frustrated with the work products. Such questions serve as early signs of potential success or failure.

Agile leaders and teams develop a comfort level with uncertainty because customers lack awareness of their needs at the outset. A collaborative, step-by-step process addresses sound design and technical needs, aligning customer and team goals. Even bad ideas are an acceptable starting point because they help teams be imaginative in creating products. The sooner the team creates an initial product output, the sooner customers respond with feedback on what they like, dislike, and why. Working together and using frequent demonstrations help teams and customers understand and solve problems.

Foster a Culture of Respect, Collaboration, and Action

Leaders encourage **calculated risks** from individuals, teams, and stake-holders, and management backing is crucial for willing employees to experiment. Such a **culture** necessitates managerial honesty and mentorship to promote team honesty, as distrust inhibits collaborative idea generation. Related to honesty is the need for workers to sense respect. When someone feels a lack of respect, they may only carry out necessary tasks, and signs of respect issues can be subtle. For instance, managers might believe they are acting respectfully, yet unawareness of a team member's background can cause unintentional disrespect. Interpretations of respect can also differ among individuals. For instance, while one person may view exciting work opportunities as a sign of respect, another might value genuine compliments more. One individual might seek a salary increase, while another may desire greater flexibility in their work hours. To inspire appropriately, a leader understands each person's preferences and acknowledges their needs.

Another aspect of organizational culture is a **bias for action**. In Agile, this means prioritizing teamwork to develop a minimally viable product and gather customer feedback early. Instead of over-planning or over-analyzing, teams decide quickly, set priorities, and act. This approach fosters experimentation and continuous improvement rather than striving for perfection. For example, suppose a leader is honest and creates an atmosphere where people respect, collaborate, and help each other stay motivated. Their bias will be toward action, and the team will work together to complete tasks. In this workplace, you can expect to see lively participation and innovation. **Effective leaders support calculated risks taken by individuals, teams, and stakeholders.**

Empower Self-Managed Teams

Agile teams are empowered and self-managed, requiring support and guidance as needed. To get the best from the team, leaders share power and understand what motivates each person. Agile teams value the concept that people conduct projects with and for people. A powerful belief in people's capabilities is key to supportive, emergent, and transformational leadership.

Agile leaders build leadership skills and confidence among team members because purposeful work leads to better customer results. Agile leaders also recognize that everyone leads in some situations. They aim to foster an environment where all individuals are self-assured when giving their viewpoints. Agile leaders encourage knowledge sharing.

Agile leaders want to establish effective working relationships with all team members and stakeholders because working together produces better results. Agile teams assess successes and challenges to refine products, people, and processes. Agile teams often reflect on what works and what does not work to improve products, people, and processes. In doing so, Agile leaders build trust, share control, and foster collaboration; they empower others to take ownership, decide, and improve together.

Lead with Clarity in Communication and Decisions

Projects are stressful undertakings, and **clear communication** is a goal and a tool for improving effectiveness in Agile. When teams communicate, they collaborate and make informed decisions, so Agile teams are often colocated. A hallmark of Agile is helping team members decide rather than deciding for them.

We encourage you to:

- **share ideas early** and get quick feedback and make improvements;
- **be transparent in communication** so everyone stays aligned and makes better decisions; and
- **let teams take ownership of decisions**, using facts, feedback, and different perspectives to find the best solutions.

Agile leaders build value through teamwork, communication, and ongoing adaptation.

Lead with Effective Communication Principles in Agile Environments

Effective communication is an integral part of Agile leadership and requires courage, consistency in truth, and timing. Good communication means listening and offering quick feedback. Agile communications use standard tools, and some are specific to Agile.

Leaders show courage by telling the truth, questioning the status quo, and having hard conversations when necessary. Dishonesty and withholding helpful information from team members and stakeholders destroys trust. When a person does not trust their leader, not much else matters. It also takes courage for team members to question norms and work practices. Challenging practices does not mean constant upheaval; it means bravely questioning whether established methods are the best. Positional leaders discuss the value of challenging practices and norms to model acceptance of this openness.

Teams often need to develop skills for handling challenging conversations. These discussions may concern inappropriate work ethics, behaviors, or communication styles. Leaders must tackle these issues, as permitting them to persist can cause harm to teamwork. It takes bravery to challenge authority, especially powerful individuals, as open-mindedness is not a universal leadership trait. Good communication is key for Agile leaders; it involves trust, challenging norms, and honest dialogue to help teams thrive.

Listen and Understand with Purpose

Conflict is inherent in teamwork, but there are distinctions between functional and dysfunctional conflicts. Disputes rooted in personalities or biases can be harmful. It is important to address these conflicts sooner rather than later. Other disagreements, such as differing opinions on work procedures, can be beneficial, as they encourage individuals to find various ways to express why their ideas are valid. Team members listen to each other's perspectives to understand why others hold their views. A neutral team member often proposes ideas for more effective solutions. The key is to keep the discussion focused on work-related issues and avoid making things personal. Creative breakthroughs often result from healthy debates on diverse ideas.

Listen to and Value All Stakeholders

It is vital to ensure stakeholders also feel **acknowledged and valued**. One strategy is to have another person rephrase what they heard. The intent is to help the team develop a shared understanding of an issue and consider different solutions on their merit. People will continue to do their best work when they perceive they are being heard, understood, and valued.

Provide Timely and Constructive Feedback

Key strengths of Agile include **transparent communication**, whereby the team quickly shares partially completed work with customers and operates in sprints. Teams use visual boards to showcase progress and gather feedback from stakeholders. Developers present their work at the end of each sprint, demonstrating the product increment to the Product Owner. Product Owners provide feedback using terms like "continue," "pivot," or "stop" (regardless of the deliverable's success at that point). Scrum Masters lead regular retrospectives where the team discusses and analyzes what worked well this time and what requires change. Then, the team selects one or two specific actions to improve upon as they "sprint" toward the final product.

Create Clear Communication Channels

Keep communication channels open. Information is powerful, and a negative perspective on this is that some individuals withhold information until it benefits them to disclose it (information and knowledge hoarding). As power imbalances can erode trust if one person believes another has more information, on Agile teams, members share information openly and frequently. Good communication shows stakeholders that the team understands the issues and is working to find solutions.

Communication Tools

Agile teams use various **communication tools**, some of which are employed in other contexts. In this section, we introduce several essential tools for Agile and clarify how these tools interconnect. Most of these tools have multiple names, but we will use the most commonly recognized ones, many of which define "ready" and "done." The tools we will discuss include:

- stand-up meetings,
- product roadmaps,
- personas with user stories,
- Kanban boards or storyboards, and
- 3 C's process of task cards.

Stand-up meetings are not unique to Agile, but they have been widely adopted in various management contexts. At daily/weekly stand-up meetings, teams discuss past work, current plans, and roadblocks. These team meetings focus on work coordination and problem identification because problem-solving happens later.

A **product roadmap** lays out the key features of work that the team expects to address in each upcoming period. For example, the team may schedule significant product releases every 6 months if a project is 2 years long. This tentative plan helps team members and the Product Owner prioritize work products.

Teams often create *personas* to visualize how their customers will use the products. These personas are real or fictional people by name, stating useful demographic information about them. For example, an Agile team may have a persona for Juan Rodriguez, age 31, who likes to play online games in the evening to unwind. Then, the team creates user stories to more precisely describe what functions and features this persona wants and why. Perhaps Juan likes to play online games building cities and is interested in native plants. The related user story may be "As a gamer, I want regional plant data for realistic city building."

The team then creates a **Kanban or storyboard**. This visual board has three columns: "to do," "in progress," and "done." The "to do" column will house the initial stories the Product Owner prioritizes. The team plans their work for the next sprint by committing to several stories and moving them into the "in-progress" column. At the end of the sprint, the Product Owner tests the work products and pushes the completed ones into the "done" column.

Each user story uses the **3 C's** model of the **card, conversation, and confirmation** to ensure understanding.

- Someone writes the user story on a card that is moved between columns as work begins and finishes.
- The team discusses the story (conversation) to confirm their understanding of what to do. The card's "ready" status means the team's work can begin. The team asks for clarifications, additional time, or resources as the work product takes shape.
- The Product Owner determines "done" to confirm the complete work.

The tools work as a system and each tool helps team members and other stakeholders understand what needs to be done, why, and the status. Agile leaders need to be comfortable with these tools and related processes.

We encourage you to:

- **listen** to understand different perspectives and foster constructive discussions, especially when conflicts arise;
- **build trust** by embracing open, honest, and timely communication, even when conversations are difficult;
- **use Agile** tools like daily stand-up meetings and Kanban boards to keep everyone informed; and
- **challenge the status quo** with courage, question existing practices, and create space for innovation.

Good communication is key for Agile leaders to build trust and collaboration.

Key Roles in Agile Leadership

Agile leadership includes key roles, and while some organizations label and define these roles differently, we will use typical titles and definitions. Also, one person may have two roles in some projects. This section defines each role and outlines helpful behaviors, and later chapters provide more details. Role descriptions are from multiple sources, including, for example:

- Anantatmula, Vittal S., and Timothy J. Kloppenborg. 2021. *Be Agile, Do Agile.* New York: Business Expert Press
- Kloppenborg, Timothy J., and Laurence J. Laning. 2012. *Strategic Leadership of Portfolio and Project Management.* New York: Business Expert Press
- Kloppenborg, Timothy J., Arthur Shriberg, and Jayashree Venkatraman. 2003. *Project Leadership.* New York: Business Expert Press

First, we will define each typical role in a sentence and then outline the key behaviors that support each role. The first three roles (sponsor, Product Owner, and Scrum Master) are complementary and distinct. The sponsor's function is at the strategic level, the Product Owner is the bridge between stakeholders and the team, and the Scrum Master works with the team.

Sponsor

Sponsors represent the project to senior management and client representatives. Sponsors provide resources, liaise with executives, make key decisions, and share responsibility for outcomes. The sponsor reports to a governing board, and many sponsors are members of these boards. One of the sponsor's roles is to keep influential board members appraised of all progress and issues. The sponsor also makes many major go/no-go project decisions. The project manager shares this responsibility with the sponsor for plan-driven projects, but in Agile, the Product Owner and the team share this responsibility.

Executives view sponsorship roles as valuable proving grounds, but busy schedules can hinder timely participation decisions. Before Agile, one author suggested that the project executive sponsor appoint an assistant to the project team. In this example, success required the executive to empower the assistant to decide on their behalf. Advocacy from sponsors is crucial for project success.

Product Owner

The *Product Owner* represents the project to the other stakeholders. The Product Owner represents and communicates with all stakeholders, prioritizes work, decides, and verifies that project deliverables meet the definition of "done." The Product Owner replaces the sponsor role in many organizations, but both exist in other organizations. When a sponsor is involved, we define which decisions remain with the sponsor and which are the Product Owner's responsibility. A key Product Owner role is to be present with the team, sometimes even daily, and to be available on short notice for decision making.

The Product Owner helps the team understand what stakeholders want. The Product Owner decides which stakeholder desires the team will satisfy first. The saying "**Eat your dessert first**" guides the team. Just as dessert is the best part of a meal for many, Agile teams start with the most crucial work to maximize customer and business value. Then they work down the priority list. At some point, the Product Owner may decide that the team has developed enough capabilities to complete the project, even if some users still want additional features.

Each iteration starts with prioritized work, capacity planning, and defining "done." That definition specifies how to assess the effectiveness of the created output. The Product Owner bridges stakeholders and the team, ensuring priorities are clear, decisions are timely, and deliverables meet expectations.

Scrum Master (Scrum Expert/Scrum Lead)

In this book, we will view **project managers** as Scrum Masters. Plan-driven project work throughout the life cycle still needs to be completed. However, when the team is engaged, the project manager's role aligns with that of the Scrum Master. The **Scrum Master** works with the team and helps the team improve, solve problems, and succeed. A Scrum Master is like a project manager but focuses on leading team discussions instead of making all the decisions. Agile teams do the same planning and control as project managers in plan-driven projects, but there are two important differences. In plan-driven projects, the project team develops the plan before starting the project, but Agile teams do much of the planning iteratively. There, data availability dictates team decision timing, which Agile teams strive to make "at the last responsible moment." The second difference is that the project manager decides on plan-driven projects, but in Agile, the team works together to decide.

A significant part of the Scrum Master's role is removing roadblocks so team members can work. Scrum Masters are often colocated with team members, which enables them to help the team solve problems quickly. Scrum Masters seek ways to improve people, products, and processes (skills, knowledge, and teamwork). Scrum Masters conduct **retrospectives** after each iteration, perhaps every 2 weeks. For effective retrospectives, teams benefit from concentrating on one improvement idea. Besides the end-of-iteration retrospectives, Scrum Masters lead their teams in daily stand-up meetings. Scrum Masters support high-performing teams by removing roadblocks, guiding decision making, and promoting continuous improvement.

Engaged Team Members

Team members collaborate to solve problems, create products, decide, and deliver solutions. Agile principles guide their work, and they work as self-organizing, cross-functional teams.

Stakeholders

There are many **stakeholders** on projects, and a project decision, activity, or outcome affects stakeholders, such as customers, users, vendors, suppliers, and the public. For example, a highway construction project involves stakeholders from the government, owners, contractors, designers, and local people and businesses.

Additional Agile Team Roles

Some organizations define and use the roles of project manager, subject matter expert (SME), functional manager, project executive, and steering committee. The titles and responsibilities of these individuals and groups vary, but we will state some of the more typical work they perform.

An **SME** is an authority on a technology, process, or business. This individual facilitates discussions and frequently makes decisions in that area. A well-known SME role in plan-driven projects is that of a business analyst who defines what will bring value to the receiving client. Business analysts confirm solutions meet expectations and requirements. Agile teams often share the Product Owner's responsibilities, but some companies use dedicated business analysts. Occasionally, someone with a different title, such as an architecture owner, may fulfill this role in Agile. In plan-driven projects, organizations often engage SMEs because multiple projects require one person's extensive knowledge, limiting their availability to part-time work for each. In some plan-driven projects, an SME contributes ideas regarding a specific issue and performs that work, but does not have decision-making authority. In contrast, Agile projects encourage team decision making.

Functional managers are the permanent heads of departments within an organization, and most team members report to a functional manager. Managers hold significant influence because they control the work of their personnel and conduct performance reviews, regardless of team connections. Agile encourages organizations to maintain stable project teams for extended periods. In such cases, team members often feel as much loyalty to their projects as they do to their functional departments. In certain organizations, such as construction companies, project managers report to a project executive, who typically has project managers as their sole direct reports. Project executives mentor project managers, share best practices, and attend progress meetings to ensure projects remain on schedule.

Finally, there is often a **governing body**. This group could be permanent (like the CEO and their team) or temporary (a project team).

In Agile, a "Release Train" is a cross-functional team of Agile teams that coordinates the predictable flow of product releases. In large organizations, these teams ensure multiple teams collaborate toward shared goals.

Project teams comprise members with diverse roles and responsibilities and well-defined roles enable teams to remain flexible and effective.

We encourage you to:

- **clarify roles** and ensure everyone understands their responsibilities to keep teams effective;
- **foster collaboration** and create a space where team members share ideas and decide together;
- **remove obstacles** and help clear roadblocks so teams can stay focused and productive; and
- **support growth** and promote feedback and continuous learning to strengthen leadership at all levels.

To succeed in Agile, leaders understand their roles and empower teams.

Adapt Leadership Styles for Agile Success

In this book, we describe three Agile leadership styles. Transformational leadership defines leading from the front. We define leading from the middle as servant leadership. We center on developmental leadership, meaning informally leading from the back. Product Owners often use transformational leadership, while Scrum Masters use servant leadership. However, regardless of role, all leaders need to use each of the three styles at least sometimes. Every leadership style serves a purpose.

Inspire Change with Transformational Leadership

The transformational leader's primary goal is to lead their team and stakeholders with a final product vision. When leaders lead by example, and everyone contributes, more gets accomplished. Transformational leaders communicate their vision and inspire followers. Such a leader is often charismatic, discussing the desired outcomes passionately and clearly. This approach spans long-term and short-term perspectives. The long-term focus reminds team members and other stakeholders of the value and excitement of their goal. The short-term perspective acknowledges progress toward that goal, even when the progress is incremental.

The transformational leader helps everyone see how their actions contribute to the larger goal. They recognize the needs and desires of each follower, helping individuals stay engaged and committed. Transformational leaders foster collaboration, encouraging everyone to work together. They view challenges as opportunities for growth rather than obstacles. This leadership style proves most effective during times of significant change (Table 3.1). **A transformational leader asks themselves, "How can I inspire my team and stakeholders to achieve our goals?"**

Support Teams with Servant Leadership

The servant leader's primary goal is to help people do their jobs. A supportive leader's primary focus is short term (on getting work done). They eliminate work obstacles and put followers' needs ahead of their own. These supportive leaders practice shared management, collaboration, and

Table 3.1 Effective transformational leadership behaviors

Vision behaviors	Outcome behaviors	Commitment behaviors	Progress behaviors
Define the vision	Commit to delivering successful outcomes	Help team members commit to outcomes	Prepare for uncertainty
Guide actions, decisions, and conversations by vision	Set clear goals, align energy toward them, and monitor progress	Engage team members in setting expectations and defining objectives	Be willing to experiment and adapt based on results
Daily, share the passionate vision with many	Prioritize the most critical outcomes first	Share authority to the extent possible	Hold self and team accountable for progress toward goals
Strive to build trust and help everyone commit to the vision	Be willing to reprioritize if some activities do not contribute to success	Secure adequate resources to implement the decisions	Describe desired outcomes with passion and clarity

enhancing the respect given to everyone. They understand that being respected encourages people's dedication to their work.

Servant leadership concepts come from two schools of thought. One is servant leadership, as popularized by Greenleaf (1998), which states that leaders' primary role is to serve those who report to them. The other is from Ubuntu, as spearheaded by Mandela and Tutu, highlighting community power during the struggles against apartheid in South Africa. A servant builds a foundation of trust and empowerment, supports the team, and helps users implement solutions (Table 3.2). **A servant leader asks themselves, "How can I serve my team and other stakeholders so that we can jointly achieve our goals?"**

Grow People Through Developmental Leadership

A developmental leader's goal is to foster individual and organizational growth informally. They lead by creating trust and hope and use their

Table 3.2 *Effective servant leader behaviors*

Culture behaviors	Communication behaviors	Accountability behaviors	Courage behaviors
Cultivate a culture built on trust, transparency, and flexibility	Communicate with integrity	Conduct hard conversations when necessary	Encourage people to act with courage instead of fear
Foster community among your team and stakeholders	Listen for understanding and empathy	Provide timely feedback so people trust you and make improvements	Support, trust, and challenge one another with respect
Keep your ethics, vision, values, and goals in constant focus	Build effective working relationships with team members	Focus on people and relationships, solving conflicts	Promote honesty so that all people feel comfortable discussing their difficulties
Create a work-life balance for yourself and help others do so	Encourage team members to share— even daily what they did, what they plan to do, and the challenges they foresee		

experience to help others grow. These leaders develop themselves first so they can help others. They build strong relationships with teammates and stakeholders, often uncovering hidden talents.

Developmental leaders support their teams behind the scenes and let others lead. These leaders help their followers gain knowledge, skills, and confidence to lead. They provide opportunities for emergent leaders. Developmental leaders foster a culture of experimentation, allowing for occasional failures and continuous learning. They work to help their team self-develop and cascade growth and learning throughout the organization.

Developmental leaders help others grow within and across organizations, including supply chains, and across the board (Table 3.3). **A developmental leader asks themselves, "How can I help develop all of my team members and other stakeholders so they can improve themselves and help others improve?"**

Table 3.3 Effective behaviors demonstrated by developmental leaders

Openness behaviors	Individual development behaviors	Encouragement behaviors	Team development behaviors
Create a climate of respect that is safe and nonjudgmental	Develop and apply one's talents	Foster informal leadership, allowing different individuals to lead at different times	Help the team develop basic agreements on how they will function
Be worthy of trust through consistent behavior	Identify the abilities of members	Encourage members to leave their comfort zones	Help the team develop shared ownership
Share incomplete thoughts and work and encourage others to do so also	Help everyone develop their talents and confidence	Hold ourselves, teams, and individuals accountable for improvement	Help team members develop critical thinking
Demonstrate empathy when dealing with people who are struggling	Provide developmental opportunities		Empower team members to make decisions and show leadership

We encourage you:

- **adapt your leadership style,** transformational, servant, or developmental, based on what your team needs most.
- **learn when to lead** from the front, support from the middle, or step back to let others grow.
- **communicate** a clear, shared vision and celebrate progress to inspire commitment.
- **remove obstacles, build trust, and create a supportive environment** where teams thrive.
- **give others meaningful opportunities** to lead and support their growth through feedback and reflection.
- **foster a culture of** experimentation and continuous learning to drive team innovation.

Agile leaders use a mix of transformational, servant, and developmental styles to meet team needs.

This chapter covers Agile methods, communication in Agile, and leadership styles for complex problems. Agile teams solve issues quickly, focusing on customer needs and improvement. We discuss the key team roles (sponsor, Product Owner, Scrum Master, and team member) and effective communication. **This chapter shows how honesty and teamwork help self-managed teams and teach leadership skills for Agile work.**

The next chapter explains how developmental leaders support and empower their teams.

Embrace the opportunity to put these principles into your leadership practice.

Empowerment is not about control—it is about creating the space for teams to adapt, learn, and thrive—start today by fostering an environment where growth and innovation take center stage.

Learn, Reflect, and Grow

Everyone has a unique way of learning and identifying areas for growth. As outlined at the end of Chapter 1, we encourage you to keep a journal. Improving skills is easier through experiential learning—"knowing, doing, and reflecting" (Kolb 2014). Review the following formats for ideas on journal topics:

- **What do I know?**
- **What am I doing?**
- **What am I reflecting on?**
- **What do we know?**
- **What are we doing?**
- **What are we reflecting on?**

This cycle is about improvement and change (Figure 3.2). It is a cycle of personal and team growth and development. Cultivating current and future leaders leaves a legacy of growth that continues to inspire and develop others. **Shared leadership is a collective responsibility.**

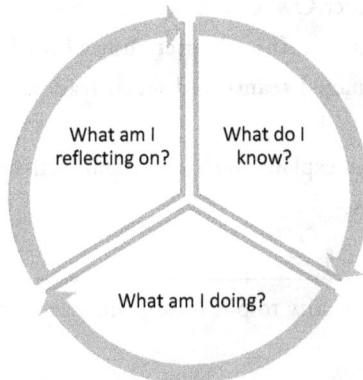

Figure 3.2 The experiential learning process (Kolb 2014)

CHAPTER 4

Developmental Leadership: Lead from Behind to Empower Others

The only thing that matters is what we do or omit to do for other people.

—George (2010, 49)

Figure 4.1 shows developmental leadership overlaps Agile leadership but offers additional ideas.

Learning Goals

- **Explain** how self-development contributes to leadership potential and enhances team performance.
- **Compare** the impact of transformational, servant, and developmental leadership styles on team dynamics and outcomes.
- **Apply** developmental leadership strategies to empower and support team members and stakeholders.
- **Develop** a personal leadership plan that aligns with core values and fosters the growth of emerging leaders.

Introduction

The previous chapter (Chapter 3) explores Agile techniques, communication, and leadership styles. With a focus on customers and continuous improvement, Agile teams find creative solutions to problems.

This chapter discusses developmental leadership and emphasizes essential leadership qualities and values to help team members

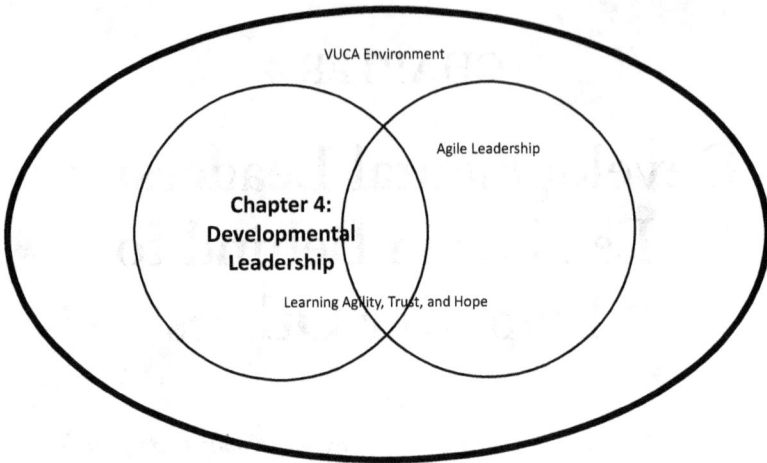

Figure 4.1 Developmental Agile Leadership roadmap

maximize their potential. Leadership development is a continuous journey, from self-awareness to empowering others. **Self-reflection helps Developmental Agile Leaders develop themselves and others.**

We begin with an overview of project governance, the project life cycle, and leadership styles related to the life cycle.

Adapt Leadership Styles to Fit Team and Project Needs

From strategy down, project management governance spans programs and portfolios. This level includes those working as program managers, portfolio managers, and senior-level sponsors. Project governance has close ties to the executive level and operational level of the organization. For example, a project management office might offer training and support. Project governance leaders approve, fund, and stage-gate projects through the life cycle. Recall that on Agile projects, this individual is the sponsor who makes important decisions. At the project level, the Product Owner represents the stakeholders and their wants and needs. This person works with the team and prioritizes project work for each iteration. The Scrum Master (project manager) is a project squad member who removes roadblocks so the squad can work to create deliverables. The Scrum Master improves processes, products, and people.

Understand Project Stages

Consider the four **project stages**: initiate, plan, execute, and close. To initiate a project, a division or department develops a business case for the proposed initiative and outlines the benefits and value. If approved, the business case forms the genesis of the project. The project team develops the project charter in the initiation stage, which will serve as the approval needed to move into the planning stage. To successfully start a project and help team members grow simultaneously, leaders will often ask teams to show how they will create successful results while using suitable methods and care for people.

Integrity capacity involves managing **complexity** to deliver results, adhering to rules, empathizing with stakeholders (even if not protected by rules), and operating within a supportive system development. Think of integrity capacity as spanning business justifications and interpersonal justifications. For example, project charters involve multiple justifications. One is the return on investment the project may generate, and another justification relates to how the project aligns with organizational goals. Besides the managerial justifications concretely outlined in the charter, projects often include justifications related to interpersonal and team conduct, such as how the team will conduct meetings, decide, and conduct themselves with moral **responsibility** in the interest of their stakeholders. Moral responsibility also includes caring for others and in how we respectfully treat one another, despite differing interpretations of respect. Integrity capacity can also span **emotional** appeals. One author prioritized emotional appeals as a project justification when working at a children's hospital on a project related to infant lives. Such justifications show stakeholder concern, and teams often show concern for team members by outlining operational procedures, including decision-making processes, meeting formats, and respectful team interactions.

In the planning stage, the project plan includes detailed estimates to develop the schedules, budgets, deliverables, and milestones. Then, the project team moves to the execution stage and spends resources and effort. At project closeout, the team completes much of the documentation, makes the last payments, and closes contracts. This stage includes project lessons learned and the products and services delivered to the end customer. The project team monitors and controls the project throughout.

Explore Leadership Styles

Table 4.1 highlights key concepts specific to the three **leadership types** (styles) and related project roles.

Now, visualize the three leadership styles throughout the project life cycle. **Transformational leaders** lead from the front (or top-level). Project leaders introduce the project to the team. In this stage, the leaders help teams and team members start the work. The leadership team makes sure the project aligns with the company's goals. With centralized power, the leadership team can set the budget and stage-gate the project through the life cycle.

Next, **servant leaders** lead from the middle. They work between the project managers, participants, and stakeholders to ensure team members can do their job. The project manager is supportive and cooperative. This person helps solve problems that come up while planning and executing projects. In keeping with the servant leader's focus on teamwork and project work, the leader ensures that the project moves in the right direction. Servant leaders support their teams and foster collaboration, shared

Table 4.1 Leadership styles, focus, authority, and impact

	Transformational leadership	Servant leadership	Developmental leadership
Leads from	The front	The middle	Behind
Description	Visionary Strategic Directs	Supportive Cooperative Facilitates	Guides Facilitates Empowers Builds relationships
Unit of focus	Organization	Team and project	Individual
Extent of power	High and centralized	Medium and shared	Unimportant Influence is key
Role examples	Project sponsor Program manager Portfolio manager	Scrum Master Project manager	Product manager Project manager Scrum Master Team member

decisions, and constructive conflict resolution. Teamwork and shared power lead to successful projects and happy customers.

> *We wish to promote a* **"bias for action"***; self-appointed leaders can achieve this by facilitating rapid decisions.* We value employees who are proactive, creative, and get results. Creativity develops innovative ideas, and innovation makes them happen.

An emphasis on action is clear through **developmental leadership**. Leadership development happens from behind because it focuses on emergence. Transformational and servant leadership center on teams and projects; developmental leadership prioritizes individual growth. Unlike transformational and servant leadership approaches, which involve degrees of positional power, power is unimportant for growth-oriented leadership. Developmental leaders use their influence with individual team members to foster their emerging leadership. Team participants and team leaders, seeing potential, encourage these emerging leaders.

We describe developmental leadership as a partnership with a trusted mentor. Nurturing leadership involves the work that occurs one-to-one in a trusting and respectful environment. In developmental leadership, a leader offers tailored guidance, nudges, feedback, and leadership task/role opportunities. Developmental leaders foster a safe, supportive environment for risk-taking. For example, the developmental leader allows a team member to chair a project status meeting. In doing so, the member gains experience managing meeting dynamics. During projects, team members emerge as leaders at their own pace.

The developmental leader knows that active involvement by many is a key to success. When several team members take the initiative as emergent leaders, the team performs better than when it relies on one leader. Much of this leadership is informal, with different people leading at various times.

One author's non-profit board experiences on worker-owned businesses illustrate promoting a bias for action. Two participants of each worker-owned business served on the board of directors as part of our developmental efforts. One firm was a janitorial service. The worker-owner janitors attended each monthly meeting, attentive but silent. The board's esteemed members—a lawyer, professor, priest, and nun—left the janitors feeling intimidated. The author mentored them for 2 years, helping them gain the confidence to speak up. The board found the developmental leadership support given to the janitors invaluable. These two individuals understood their industry the best and when they shared their experiences, the board made better decisions. The two individuals expressed how the developmental process helped them feel heard and valued, and built their confidence in expressing their ideas at board meetings.

Project managers use different leadership methods (transformational, servant, developmental). Developmental leadership involves acting. **As you apply leadership styles across the project life cycle, you will find different styles helpful depending on the context.**

We encourage you to:

- **understand** when to lead, support, or guide, tailoring your leadership approach to your team and the project phase;
- **promote a bias for action** and empower team members to take initiative and solve problems;
- **mentor emerging leaders** and give them opportunities to grow in a supportive environment; and
- **use a mix of leadership styles** to drive project success and help your team develop.

Insights from Developmental Leadership Research

Although invisible, values are the principles and beliefs through which we express ourselves in actions and words. Values define us, who we are, and who we want to be. The values and behaviors in this section span the project roles of the sponsor, Scrum Master, team members, and stakeholders. Note that developmental and Agile leadership involve many more values and actions than described in this chapter.

Hudson's Six Core Values of Developmental Leadership

Earlier, we introduced **virtues** such as integrity and kindness as desirable character qualities; think of virtues as **values**. We exhibit values in how we walk the talk. Hudson identified six core values of developmental leadership (1999). These values apply to self-improvement and to helping others grow.

- **Personal power** spans *self-esteem, confidence, and courage*. Leaders develop their teams by empowering each member, remaining mindful that each team member will have different developmental needs.
- **Achievement** shows *purposefulness through accomplishments*. Leaders help team members grow by providing personalized opportunities that match their skills.
- **Intimacy** involves cultivating relationships and being a friend. Developmental leaders mentor and advise team members, fostering close professional bonds.
- **Play and creativity** have to do with *imagination, spontaneity, and expression*. Developmental leaders understand that in a VUCA environment, creativity helps teams be innovative, as this leads to novel solutions. Sometimes, it helps when the entire group takes a break, relaxes, and steps away from the pressures of work.
- **Search for meaning** involves *developing inner wisdom*. Developmental leaders guide team members to develop self-awareness and understand what is meaningful to them.
- **Compassion** means *helping, improving, serving, and caring for others*. Developmental leaders prioritize others' needs to cultivate future leaders.

Gilley's Developmental Leadership Model

The **developmental leadership model** draws from research on organizational learning, change, and development (Gilley et al. 2011). The model involves being guided by core values to create a sense of purpose and foster creativity and innovation. Leadership development is based on continuous development. A developmental leader is:

- **hopeful**: This individual is trustworthy and patient and cultivates a culture of allowing individuals to fail and try again;
- **one who develops**: The person supports the team, nurtures individual growth, and builds confidence;
- **accomplished**: This person is a clear, confident, and effective communicator who follows through;
- **authentic**: This individual is honest, friendly, and optimistic;
- **fair**: This individual is open-minded, flexible, and impartial; and
- **growth mindset focused**: This person values the journey and the end goal. This leader helps prepare each person for success and lets others take credit.

Developmental Leadership and Catholic Social Teaching

Developmental leadership and **Catholic Social Teaching** (Trinity Communications, 2024) share similar ideas as the focus is on helping new leaders work toward:

- team, organization, and stakeholder well-being;
- authenticity and respect for human dignity in all;
- a recognition that all stakeholders (including oneself) have rights and accompanying responsibilities;
- decisions at the lowest level whenever possible; and
- a sense of community, solidarity, and participation by all stakeholders.

Moral development is a key part of leadership development. Individuals with low moral development use manipulation to get what they want. Individuals initially comply, fulfilling obligations minimally, marking a stage in moral growth. Top moral development ends with integrity when everyone knows the person will be honest and truthful enough to do what is right. Trust results from this level of development. As we help our team members and leaders of tomorrow develop skills, we also want to help them develop morally.

Additional Developmental Leadership Behaviors

Good values lead to better leadership, as exemplified by **behaviors** that:

- demonstrate courage in words and actions;
- avoid both perception and reality of a conflict of interest;
- use reflection before action;
- manage stress;
- approach key influencers to develop project support;
- establish trust and reciprocity with each person;
- seek help when needed;
- admit mistakes, accept blame, and ensure the same mistake does not happen again; and
- share credit.

Developmental leadership helps employees find more purpose, collaboration, and commitment.

We encourage you to:

- **lead with core values** and use integrity, confidence, and compassion to support personal and team growth;
- **foster a culture of development**, and help individuals build skills, confidence, and leadership abilities;
- **embrace a** growth **mindset** and value learning, resilience, and shared success over individual recognition; and
- **prioritize trust and** collaboration and ensure decisions are fair, authentic, and respectful of stakeholders.

The values, principles, and beliefs that ground us and represent how we lead enable us to help others create their purpose as emerging leaders.

Develop Yourself as a Leader First

Once we develop ourselves as leaders, we can help others lead.

Reflective exercises to cultivate core leadership values and behaviors

This section combines values (virtues) and behaviors and introduces several **reflective exercises**.

- Begin by reflecting on your values specific to leadership
  - ○ Identify the top three values that are most meaningful to you.
  - ○ Now, consider how you convey your values to others through your words and actions.
  - ○ Reflect on the consistency between your values and behaviors.
- Reflect on one or two individuals who most contributed to your current leadership abilities
  - ○ What actions and statements did they make? How did these practices reflect specific values?
  - ○ How consistent are their values and conduct?
  - ○ What is most meaningful?
- Identify a gap between your values and responses and those of the leaders who influenced you
  - ○ How can you close the gap to develop your values and behaviors?

These exercises assist you in defining your leadership values and, as you discuss developmental leadership with your team members and stakeholders.

Lead with Humility

Humbleness means showing humility and admitting and sharing your mistakes with others. This can serve as a reflective exercise, demonstrating to others that we are vulnerable and human. Shared experiences foster resilience, hope, and mutual support, and by modeling humility, we can help individuals and groups do the same. Reflect on how insights from your humility exercises can help you mentor others.

Lead with Commitment

When we show leadership **commitment**, we are trustworthy and inspire commitment in others. We follow through on responsibilities and promises with behaviors (actions) and deliverables. By committing to delivering results, we foster respect and trust and model leadership behaviors. Sometimes, this requires challenging assumptions and the status quo to get things done. We also show commitment by being available to team members and listening to their concerns. Reflect on how insights from your commitment exercises can help you mentor others.

Advocate for Leadership Growth

A key leadership skill is supporting your team and their work with **advocacy**. By advocating for others, you create a safe environment for them to experiment with work-related tasks. When we advocate, we show we value new ideas from everyone, including stakeholders. Reflect on how insights from your advocacy exercises can help you mentor others.

We encourage you to:

- **align your values with actions**, and ensure that your leadership is authentic, consistent, and reflective of what matters most to you;
- **build your leadership skills,** understand your strengths, improve your weaknesses, and support your team;
- **lead with humility**, acknowledge mistakes, foster resilience, and create a culture of trust and openness;
- **show commitment**, meet responsibilities, challenge assumptions, and support your team; and
- **advocate for others** and create a supportive environment where everyone feels valued and empowered.

We can help others grow and emerge as leaders through self-reflection and awareness.

Help Others Grow as Leaders

Facilitate leadership development of others and assist them in reaching their potential. Help others by sharing experiences, collaborating, and providing support.

Share the Leadership Journey

The practice of **sharing the journey** involves being there with them and for them. When we accompany others on the project journey, we show we are there for the long haul of the project and to mentor and guide them in their development. By fostering leadership development, we empower the entire team. Helping project participants make their own choices gives them control. Help them build confidence and thrive in a supportive environment where everyone feels appreciated, heard, and can share their ideas.

Help others develop agency by identifying or creating opportunities to lead on project tasks or roles. Project members might hesitate to try something new or take on a leadership role task. Support them by creating a climate of respect that is safe and nonjudgmental. Focus on building a culture of commitment and results so that team members have a sense of security as they take the brave first steps in leading project tasks.

Treat People as Individuals

Developmental leaders focus on *each team member's* growth, needs, and well-being. They help team members by listening and coaching them to achieve their goals. The developmental leader provides tailored feedback and opportunities in close collaboration with everyone. This involves training, support, and creating a positive environment for growth. Developmental leaders help people gain confidence in their abilities. This process builds resilience, improving teamwork, and collaboration.

Share Decision Making

Collaborative leadership requires a **common aim** and the distribution of decision making at a measured rate. Individual check-ins help leaders identify team members ready for more responsibilities.

Foster Leadership Growth

Developmental leadership helps team participants **grow** into self-sufficient leaders. The process involves encouraging people to leave their comfort zones. Leaders develop others by sharing experiences, personalizing support, and involving them in decisions. Developmental leaders cultivate leadership growth.

Give Personal Attention to Team Members and Stakeholders

Helping others develop their leadership takes time, effort, and **individualized attention**. Some suggested practices follow:

- *Seek to understand* others and their feelings, emotions, beliefs, and values.
- *Learn* what motivates each person to help them achieve goals.
- *Gauge* each person's feelings, emotions, beliefs, and values.
- *Hold* yourself and others accountable.
- *Respect* each other's independence to the extent practical.
- *Act as if* everyone is a volunteer who can leave if unchallenged and dissatisfied.
- *Ask* yourself, *How can I help my collaborators and constituents develop and use their leadership potential?*

Let us consider introductory, mid-level, and higher-level leadership dimensions on progression. An introductory level of using knowledge and experience to influence others may be to suggest ideas. A mid-level of ability and experience may ensure that facts and examples back the ideas one suggests. Higher knowledge and expertise may involve valuing viewpoints and shaping a more nuanced solution.

Recall that happiness is one measure of success in Agile and, while this may sound strange, it has logic. In Agile, a happy team means everyone senses appreciation and acceptance. You want stakeholders to be enthusiastic about the project and help champion it in their interactions with others. Their happiness hinges on a workable plan and the belief that it will succeed. Believing their work is purposeful makes people working on the project happy. If they are unhappy, their work may lack purpose, the overall direction may seem senseless, or they may experience overwork and stress. These issues foreshadow project difficulties, so ensure that project collaborators are enthusiastic and motivated.

We encourage you to:

- **accompany others on their leadership journey**—be present, mentor them, and create space for them to lead;
- **recognize and support each person's** unique strengths, needs, and motivations;
- **share decision making** by building trust and promoting collaborative leadership;
- **nurture growth** by offering stretch opportunities, timely guidance, and a safe space to learn; and
- **personalize your leadership approach to foster confidence, agency, and leadership potential in every team member.**

Developing others as leaders creates a stronger, more capable team built on trust, collaboration, and shared success.

Chapter 4 emphasizes personal and team potential, covering project management, leadership styles, and self-development. It shows how sharing experiences and communication helps colleagues and stakeholders become leaders. This chapter provides a framework for guiding others in their growth, helping them find purpose and step into leadership roles. **Developmental leadership fosters an environment where everyone can thrive and contribute to team success.**

Embrace the opportunity to put these principles into your leadership practice.

True leadership means walking alongside others, guiding from behind, and ensuring that every voice is heard and every potential is realized—not leading from the front.

The next chapter discusses how leaders build teams that learn, adapt, and collaborate.

Learn, Reflect, and Grow

Everyone has a unique way of learning and identifying areas for growth. As outlined at the end of Chapter 1, we encourage you to keep a journal. Improving skills is easier through experiential learning— "knowing, doing, and reflecting" (Kolb, 2014). Review the following formats for ideas on journal topics:

- **What do I know?**
- **What am I doing?**
- **What am I reflecting on?**
- **What do we know?**
- **What are we doing?**
- **What are we reflecting on?**

This cycle is about improvement and change (Figure 4.2). It is a cycle of personal and team growth and development. Cultivating current and future leaders leaves a legacy of growth that continues to inspire and develop others. **Shared leadership is a collective responsibility.**

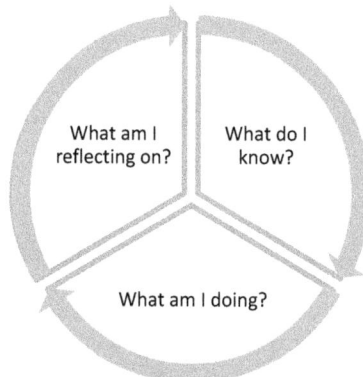

Figure 4.2 The experiential learning process (Kolb 2014)

PART 2

Implement Developmental Agile Leadership Practices

CHAPTER 5

Inspire Teams and Stakeholders to Learn and Improve Together

We now accept the fact that learning is a lifelong process of keeping abreast of change. And the most pressing task is to teach people how to learn.
—Drucker (1993, 49)

Figure 5.1 shows that many of the actions leaders can take to inspire team and stakeholder learning come from Agile leadership, but some come from developmental leadership.

Developmental Agile Leadership is a fulfilling journey of personal growth and effectiveness, empowering individuals, teams, and stakeholders to lead, especially during turbulent times. By cultivating your leadership skills and strengths and sharing leadership, you empower others to step into their leadership potential.

> Developmental leadership + Agile = Developmental Agile Leadership

Learning Goals

- **Identify** the role of stakeholder-centered leadership in enhancing engagement and project outcomes.
- **Describe** how trust, hope, and stakeholder needs influence team culture and performance.
- **Apply** feedback and learning agility to improve collaboration and drive continuous improvement.
- **Develop** a leadership strategy that promotes team agility, growth, and shared learning.

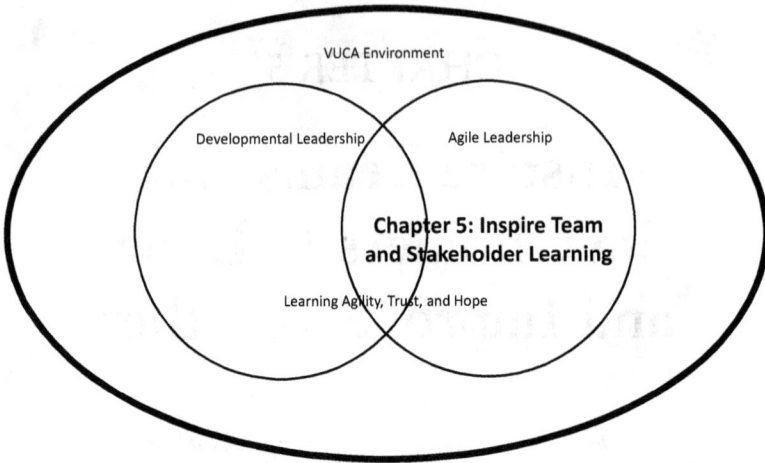

Figure 5.1 Developmental Agile Leadership roadmap

Introduction

We draw from Agile principles, in which teams learn to "be agile." Like Agile teams, this book uses an iterative process to help you develop skills. **The primary goal is to develop current and future leaders.**

This book explores three elements of Developmental Agile Leadership:

1. **Principles**: Create a stakeholder-centered culture emphasizing learning agility, trust, and hope.
2. **Mindset**: Foster continuous learning through reflection and feedback.
3. **Developmental Agile Leadership**: Apply these principles and mindset to empower individuals, cultivate leadership, and strengthen teams.

Lead with values, think and act with agility, and prioritize collaboration.

Leadership is about helping others grow—when you share, support, and adapt, you build stronger teams and future leaders.

The first half of our book explains leadership concepts. The chapters lay the foundation for leadership practices in turbulent times.

Chapter 1 covers the challenges of a changing world and leadership approaches. Developmental leadership and Agile leadership promote shared leadership through learning and adaptation.

Chapter 2 shows that learning agility, trust, and hope are key to Developmental Agile Leadership.

Chapter 3 explores Agile leadership priorities, communication principles, and leadership roles and styles. With a focus on customers and improvement, Agile teams find creative solutions to problems. Chapters 2 and 3 set the stage for helping teams and stakeholders learn together, as detailed in Chapter 5.

Chapter 4 focuses on Developmental Agile Leadership and explains that the process begins with self-development. Learn how leaders drive team growth and create customer value in Chapters 5 to 7, where we discuss implementation practices.

This chapter is on inspiring teams and stakeholders. Teamwork requires a common purpose, motivation, and effectiveness of each member. **By aligning leadership practices with stakeholder needs and embracing Agile techniques, leaders empower teams to learn, adapt, and lead effectively together.**

Chapter 6 offers practical suggestions for team and stakeholder engagement. The process includes improving team meetings, decisions, conflict resolution, and stakeholder relationships.

Chapter 7 describes how leaders cultivate emergent leadership and develop the leaders of tomorrow. The goal is to build a leadership culture of shared growth and empowerment.

Chapter 8 concludes by bringing it all together with our hope that this book empowers you to navigate a complex world with resilience. We hope you use the ideas in this book to enhance your leadership and help others reach their potential.

Build a Stakeholder-Centered Leadership Culture

Leaders develop themselves, promote skilled teams, and build a customer-focused culture.

Align Leadership Development with Stakeholder Needs

As they develop themselves and others, leaders *align* personal growth and that of their followers to stakeholders' needs. Effective leaders show humility when establishing relationships with their team members and stakeholders. Agile leaders empower others and treat everyone individually. People listen to them because they listen to others, keep their promises, and lead teams and stakeholders toward desired outcomes. These leaders create an adaptive, growth-focused environment. This alignment ensures project outcomes meet stakeholder needs.

Develop an Adaptive, Growth-Focused Culture

Leaders' self-improvement fosters a **culture** of active engagement among teams and involved parties. This builds trust and collaboration among teams and stakeholders. Leaders show reciprocity by modeling:

- **honesty**, including sharing bad and challenging news;
- **respect** for everyone;
- **motivation**, such that everyone wants the project to succeed;
- **collaboration** between individuals and stakeholders;
- **a bias for action** instead of awaiting direction; and
- **ethical conduct.**

Keep Stakeholders' Needs at the Center of Leadership Decisions

Project success hinges on understanding and responding to **stakeholders' needs.** To serve stakeholders well, leaders solicit feedback early and often

Table 5.1 Stakeholder-related leadership actions

Build relationships and trust	Plan in collaboration	Create useful outcomes
Establish genuine two-way communication	Establish a shared vision with stakeholders	Align actions and behaviors to satisfy needs and desires
Lead associates, customers, and suppliers in an empowering style	Clarify client desires and treat them as expectations	Make and facilitate necessary decisions embracing changes clients prefer
Work with stakeholders to understand their needs	Set a clear direction for further planning and execution	Develop a shared understanding of risk
Encourage stakeholder participation for actionable input	Prioritize among competing objectives	Manage issues as they arise
Develop shared ownership	Identify complex trade-offs and their consequences	Serve as stewards of parent and customer organizations

toward solution development. Table 5.1 exemplifies leadership actions to take with and for stakeholders.

Building trust and relationships is key to successful collaboration.

Most projects have many stakeholders; the first step is identifying and understanding their concerns. Some stakeholders are internal, others are external; some care about the project process, while others care about the project deliverables. On most projects, there are many stakeholders with conflicting desires and understandings.

Next, project teams strive to prioritize the stakeholders, as some yield more power over the project than others do. Supporters and opponents will emerge and some will remain neutral. Project teams collaborate with, influence, and seek buy-in from those affected by the project. Many project teams use spreadsheets to identify, understand, prioritize, learn from, and influence stakeholders. Table 5.2 exemplifies a stakeholder matrix.

In Table 5.2, project leaders understand they want the project goal to offer value to their clients. Early stakeholder planning helps stakeholders determine and communicate their vision of project success.

Table 5.2 Stakeholder matrix template

Stakeholder	Interest in project	Priority level (1–3)	Level of support or opposition	Collaboration and influence strategies

After identifying and prioritizing stakeholders, understanding their vested interests and concerns and working with them throughout the project becomes crucial. Experienced project leaders understand that stakeholders often have hard and soft concerns. Challenging concerns are usually quantitative and more straightforward to measure. Soft concerns are more complicated to explain and involve feelings. Regular interaction with stakeholders involves sharing ideas and deliverables (even partial deliverables) early and often to ensure teams stay on course and meet objectives.

Reinforce a Stakeholder-Centered Culture

There are many aspects to a **stakeholder-centered culture**.

We encourage you to:

- **develop** yourself and your team, build internal leadership, meet stakeholder needs, and adapt to feedback;
- **build** trust and hope by being transparent, accountable, and supportive; and
- **engage** stakeholders regularly, ensuring clear communication and shared goals.

Effective leadership prioritizes stakeholder needs through development, trust, and alignment.

Inspire Leadership Through Trust and Hope

Leaders who collaborate with teams and stakeholders to set expectations inspire everyone. Leaders create and maintain trust, so people have confidence and hope as they envision the desired future. When people are excited about a project, they work hard to see it to a successful conclusion.

Build Trust Through Leadership Actions

Trust in their leaders is crucial for individuals to thrive and challenge themselves. For example, problems can erode trust, and one mistake can lead to another. Challenges require a leader's direct attention and action, and this is where trust and hope play a vital role. Leaders build trust by delegating, providing resources, and supporting team decisions. A motivated team will outperform a less motivated team, even if the latter makes better decisions. Leaders strengthen trust by repeating the project vision and making it easy to follow.

It is important for leaders to understand everyone's needs and concerns, and open communication and respect for diverse perspectives are crucial. Help everyone experience belonging and security and maintain their confidences.

Create a Culture of Hope

Hope is when your team and stakeholders have confidence in delivering a solution. It drives relationships and fuels project success. Leaders articulate the project vision and describe how it delivers value. The vision extends beyond what teams expect to deliver—it sets the path forward and describes lasting effects on stakeholders. Leaders also commit to the vision to inspire others' commitment.

Prioritizing teamwork fosters hope and high-value deliverables follow. A central tenet of Agile is to provide value to customers early and often, starting with priority wants and needs. Early feedback helps teams and stakeholders set realistic goals and successful delivery of each increment increases overall project success.

Positive feedback boosts team members' outlook and hope helps build resilience. Teamwork also builds friendships. One friend offers this idea regarding hope and commitment:

> In difficult and complex environments, the inspiration of hope is a key component to enlisting the type of commitment necessary to achieve difficult things. The grit necessary to approach each day with energy, clarity, and passion when progress isn't linearly gained or obvious day-to-day is bolstered by the hope that we can indeed make an impact and that said impact will create a better world.
>
> —Jesse Maleszewski

Practical Ways to Strengthen Trust and Hope in Teams

Trust and hope inspire teams to **persevere** through difficulties, forming the basis of strong leadership.

We encourage you to:

- **build trust** by supporting your team, delegating responsibilities, and providing resources for success;
- **be transparent and consistent** in your actions and communications to strengthen confidence;
- **inspire hope** by showing optimism, setting a clear vision, and making personal commitments to project success;
- **foster collaboration** and celebrate progress to keep motivation high and resilience strong.

Trust and hope form the foundation of strong leadership, motivating teams to overcome challenges and stay committed to success.

Leverage Rapid Feedback for Continuous Improvement

Agile prioritizes early, frequent value delivery and rapid feedback for improvement.

Embrace Feedback and Put It into Action

Agile teams prioritize early, frequent **feedback** for continuous improvement. They work in short cycles called increments or sprints, dividing work into manageable steps. User stories help teams focus on a specific feature a customer wants. The Product Owner may decide that the first step is for the team to assess the risks involved. Can the team overcome the most significant risk? Failure to overcome the risk might lead to project cancellation or a substantial change in direction.

At the end of each sprint, a customer representative provides feedback on whether the deliverable meets satisfaction and the agreed-upon definition of "done." If so, the Product Owner will select the next highest-value item for the team to create. The team remains receptive, avoiding defensiveness if the deliverable falls short of expectations or customer satisfaction. The team discusses the gap between meeting the "done" criteria and what deficiencies led them to fail. These rapid learning cycles allow for ongoing refinement and sustain continuous improvement.

The team uses feedback to improve and make data-backed choices. This approach also applies to partial ideas so others can understand different thought processes. Ongoing dialogue and collaboration foster better results. Clear, documented information and sharing implicit knowledge improve learning within teams and organizations.

Another hallmark of Agile stems from Deming's (1986) classic **continuous improvement model** of plan–do–check–act model, as per Figure 5.2.

As team members and stakeholders work together to deliver quality results, they rely on each other's experiences and input when planning tasks. The approach involves using processes that have worked before and focusing on improving one work activity at a time. These improvements happen in short, focused cycles.

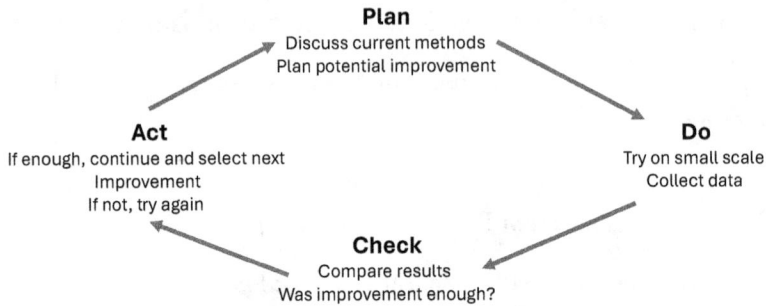

Figure 5.2 Continuous improvement cycle

While stakeholders set the standards for what is acceptable, the team assesses the process. If the results meet expectations, the team continues with the same approach. If not, the team tries a different method, aiming for better results. However, the success of this cycle is not automatic—it depends on individual actions. Leaders play a role by modeling, listening, observing, and reflecting behaviors. Safe work environments foster learning from mistakes, and leaders who support incremental changes minimize the risk of major errors.

Concepts from Chapter 2, where we stress a **growth mindset**, aid in reframing setbacks as part of learning. Leaders can foster this mindset by being open regarding their challenges and sharing their lessons. Project teams ask:

- What went wrong and why?
- What worked and why?
- What can we improve next time?

This helps identify areas for growth and is also a time to celebrate achievements. Trust builds successful teamwork—enough confidence to share mistakes and learn. By doing so, teams and stakeholders form a learning community and continue to improve by learning from successes and mistakes.

Strengthen Team and Stakeholder Collaborative Learning

Product Owners, sponsors, and Scrum Masters can **boost team and stakeholder learning** with these actions.

We encourage you to:

- **clarify risks early** by involving stakeholders and surfacing concerns across the project;
- **encourage open conversations about conflict**—lean into discomfort to uncover deeper insights;
- **run short learning cycles to test solutions**, evaluate results, and adapt decisions collaboratively;
- **model curiosity** by asking powerful questions, reflecting openly, and sharing lessons learned.

Continuous feedback fuels improvement, enabling teams to refine their work and deliver greater value. **Leaders who encourage learning, open communication, and safe experimentation improve teams.**

To conclude, this chapter details the practical application of concepts from Chapter 2 on trust, hope, and learning agility. It shows Agile practices from Chapter 3 and highlights a stakeholder-driven culture. This chapter emphasizes implementing Developmental Agile Leadership practices. **These practices help teams work better together, learn from errors, and make progress.**

Embrace the opportunity to put these principles into your leadership practice.

A growth mindset culture starts with you—lead by example, encourage curiosity, and create an environment where learning and leadership flourish hand in hand.

The next chapter discusses Developmental Agile Leadership to enable teams and stakeholders.

Learn, Reflect, and Grow

Everyone has a unique way of learning and identifying areas for growth. As outlined at the end of Chapter 1, we encourage you to keep a journal. Improving skills is easier using the experiential learning process—"knowing, doing, and reflecting" (Kolb 2014). Review the following formats for ideas on journal topics:

- **What do I know?**
- **What am I doing?**
- **What am I reflecting on?**
- **What do we know?**
- **What are we doing?**
- **What are we reflecting on?**

This cycle is about improvement and change (Figure 5.3). It is a cycle of personal and team growth and development. Cultivating current and future leaders leaves a legacy of growth that continues to inspire and develop others. **Shared leadership is a collective responsibility.**

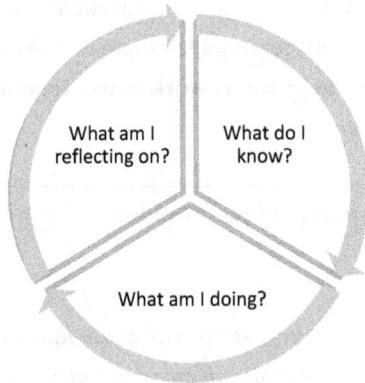

Figure 5.3 The experiential learning process (Kolb 2014)

CHAPTER 6

Developmental Agile Leadership in Action: Enable Teams and Stakeholders

Alone we can do so little; together we can do so much.
—Keller (1999, 123)

Figure 6.1 demonstrates that many of the actions leaders can take to enable their teams and stakeholders come from Agile leadership and some come from developmental leadership.

Learning Goals

- **Identify** project risks and categorize them based on likelihood and impact.
- **Describe** conflict resolution strategies that can improve teamwork and collaboration.
- **Apply** communication techniques to strengthen stakeholder engagement and improve team alignment.

- **Develop** a leadership approach that encourages self-managed teams and supports decision making.

Introduction

Chapter 5 explains how Agile teams develop and support a growth mindset culture (where the team learns and leads together) and builds a learning culture.

This chapter expands on this with Agile concepts and practices that empower teams and stakeholders to succeed. The chapter explores

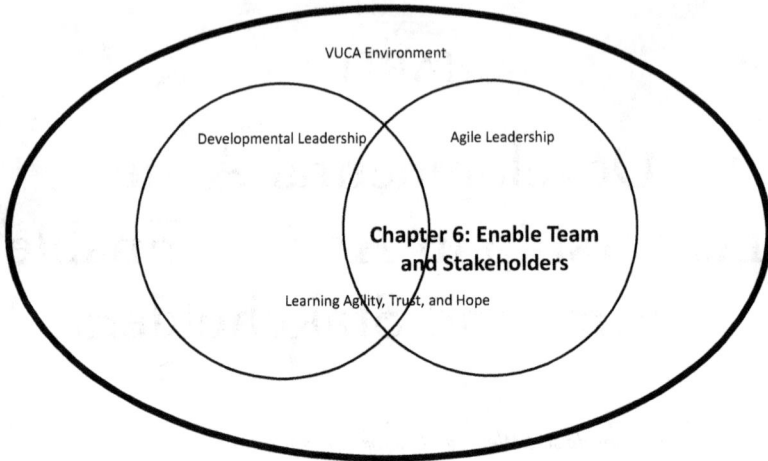

Figure 6.1 Developmental Agile Leadership roadmap

key practices for managing risks, resolving conflict, and fostering clear communication. Initiative-taking risk management prevents setbacks, and constructive conflict strengthens ideas and relationships. Agile teams thrive on open communication, efficient meetings, and structured decision making. As teams mature into self-managed teams, they become more engaged, innovative, and resilient. **These practices create an environment of trust and learning.**

Understand Risks and Obstacles

Creating something new involves many challenges. In Agile leadership, teams first identify and prioritize project risks before they address the most significant ones. Throughout, they manage risks because risk management is an ongoing process.

Identify Risks Early

Early stakeholder engagement helps teams **identify** risks with prompts, such as:

- What difficulties did we experience with an earlier or similar project?
- What problems could arise in this project?
- How can others help us in identifying risks?

Teams categorize risks, for example, under such headings as resources, technology, regulations, coordination, finances, stakeholder buy-in, and weather.

Just as sports teams conduct post-game reviews to identify strengths, weaknesses, and areas for improvement, project teams use **lessons learned** to review the process, the success outcome, and client satisfaction. Agile teams are unique because they also conduct **premortems**, where they imagine the project has failed. This approach aids the team in identifying potential problem areas to plan for and manage.

Prioritize Potential Risks

Risk **prioritization** helps distribute resources and focus on critical issues. Risk evaluation considers project type, probability, and impact. For example, archaeological projects involve unique risks. One of the book's coauthors was involved in an archeological project where the team faced dangers like snakebites and drug lords. Project teams often develop a risk diagram, like the one illustrated next, to examine probabilities and impacts (Figure 6.2).

In Figure 6.2, the horizontal axis shows the potential impact if a risk occurs, while the vertical axis represents the likelihood of the risk happening. The team also draws a concave line from high probability and no impact to high impact and no probability. The team and stakeholders then assess the likelihood and impact of each risk. Risks above the line are

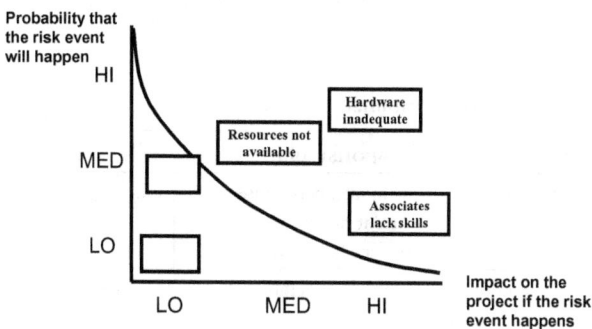

Figure 6.2 Risk probability and impact example

Adapted from Kloppenborg et al. (2023, 84–85).

of primary concern, and the team develops plans to manage them. The team addresses the risks below the line if they occur.

Respond Adaptively to Risks

Remember, a key Agile principle is to deliver **maximum value** as quickly as possible. The team selects the client's most desired feature and prioritizes it for development because risks that occur limit the project's value. If a team cannot manage a major risk, they may have to cancel or revise the project. Risk responses reduce the likelihood and impact of events. An adaptive response plan includes **pivots** (quick changes in direction).

Monitor and Manage Risks

Once a risk response plan is in place, teams **monitor** risks because continuous risk monitoring is essential to ensure effective risk management strategies. The team reviews the risk status of each risk, reevaluates priorities, and adjusts plans as needed. Monitoring also enables the team to stay ahead of potential issues. Like a meteorologist tracking the weather, the team ensures a member has **risk ownership** for each risk to watch for early warning signs of problems.

Once the risk owner identifies an imminent event, they lead the response plan. Through the Agile **swarming** process, other team members collaborate to manage the risk. This metaphor is from nature, where bees swarm and work together to protect their hives. The risk response matrix displays ownership information as exemplified (Table 6.1).

Table 6.1 Sample risk response matrix

Risk event	Response plan	Who owns the risk?
Inadequate hardware	Team members revise current hardware Replace hardware	Edie
Team members do not have the skills for key functions	Train team members Hire more people	Padraig
Key resources are unavailable	Identify an external consultant to fill the need	Ute

Adapted from Kloppenborg et al. (2023, 84–85).

Lead Risk Management for Project Success

Risk management is crucial when developing something new, as challenges and conflicts are unavoidable.

We encourage you to:

- use premortems to envision project failure and identify potential issues before they occur;
- prioritize risks and evaluate their likelihood and impact. Focus the team's efforts on the key risks first;
- assign "risk owners" to each risk to monitor for early signs of trouble and take the lead if the risk materializes; and
- swarm risks and gather the team to address them as soon as they arise.

Finding and fixing problems early helps projects run smoothly.

Navigate Conflicts for Better Outcomes

Conflict is inevitable in projects, but team growth comes from constructively managing work-related disagreements. Effective teams confront and address dysfunctional interpersonal conflict. Risk management takes courage and leaders use different conflict resolution strategies to navigate these challenges.

Functional and Dysfunctional Conflict

Teams often debate competing ideas and it is acceptable to disagree with work methods, as this is a **functional conflict**, and it improves the work. Team discussions help find better solutions by weighing the pros and cons. In contrast, interpersonal conflict is **dysfunctional** and disrupts group work and team dynamics.

Address Conflict with Courage

Opting for harmony feels safer and involves less effort, but can increase project difficulties. Standing up to unreasonable client or manager demands takes **bravery**. To prepare for difficult discussions, the team must detail why a proposed solution will not work, provide examples, and address counterarguments. The team may have to accept modifications to their work, even if they disagree. The team sets realistic goals and keeps customer priorities and feedback in mind.

Everyone makes mistakes; we are all human. As leaders cultivate trust and a psychologically safe environment, they acknowledge their errors. Leaders share what they have learned from their mistakes and how they continue to develop to encourage team members to do the same.

Choose the Proper Conflict Resolution Strategy

Table 6.2 shows several conflict resolution methods.

Keep in mind that each technique suits different circumstances. Although teamwork is effective for decisions that require everyone's support, it takes time. Sometimes, compromise resolves disagreements, enabling everyone to be involved. The smoothing approach involves focusing on common ground while downplaying minor differences. Withdrawal

Table 6.2 Conflict resolution approaches

Conflict resolution approach	Definition	Best used when …
Collaboration	Work together toward a beneficial solution	Time permits; firm agreement is necessary
Compromise	Find a balanced solution where each party makes concessions	A perfect solution is unachievable; trade-offs lead to progress
Smooth it over	Downplay differences; focus on common ground	Disagreement is minor
Withdrawal	Step back from the conflict, temporarily or fully	Disagreement is minor, or withdrawing will prevent escalation
Vote	Let the majority decide with a quick vote	It helps to test the waters for agreement
Force	Make quick, top-down decisions when necessary	Urgent action is necessary; other approaches have failed

Adapted from Kloppenborg et al. (2023, 182–83).

entails postponing decisions and sometimes, it is the best option to use. A transparent voting process shows winners and losers and can affect team cohesion. However, a straw vote to gauge opinions or an anonymous vote can help propel the team toward a decision. Because imposing decisions erode team trust, morale, and empowerment, it should be a last-resort measure.

Remember, conflict is an unavoidable aspect of organizational dynamics, but effective management can improve outcomes.

Lead Conflict Resolution to Strengthen Teams

Here are some strategies to enhance leadership skills as you navigate conflicts.

We encourage you to:

- **address personal conflict** and focus on work-related conflicts to strengthen team collaboration;
- **face conflicts with courage**, address issues, and discuss solutions to keep the team on track; and
- **choose the proper conflict resolution method** based on the situation and move the team forward.

Effective conflict management fosters collaboration, strengthens teams, and turns challenges into opportunities for growth.

Communicate with Clarity and Impact

Teams and stakeholders interact frequently over the project life cycle. In Agile, the Product Owner (who represents stakeholders) meets with the team daily. Scrum Masters and Product Owners put a lot of time and effort into communications and meetings because effective communication fosters collaboration and ensures teams stay aligned. This section shows how to share information, involve stakeholders, and use Agile tools for project success.

Prioritize Clear and Effective Communication

Effective communication is essential for project success as it helps solve problems and keeps things running. **Prioritizing communication** helps teams navigate challenges, solve problems, and keep momentum.

Time constraints often require quick information sharing for prompt decisions. Although busy managers and executives prefer short, concise requests, other issues require complete, current, contextualized details to improve decisions. Use the **Goldilocks** approach to balance communication needs between too little and too much. Environments encouraging open communication and excitement allow engaged teams to thrive because it motivates people to work toward a common purpose.

Leverage Agile Communication Tools

Agile projects use various **communication tools**, depending on whether the team is colocated on-site, virtual, or hybrid. The communication matrix, Agile project roadmap, and Kanban board are three essential visual tools. Teams post these tools in a high-traffic work spot for team members and stakeholders to view easily. The communication matrix helps coordinate project communication with stakeholders, as exemplified in Table 6.3.

To fill in the matrix, the team identifies stakeholders and prioritizes them. The team figures out what information stakeholders need to provide. The third column details the team's required stakeholder communications, including project updates and issue reports. Both parties discuss issues and concerns. The fourth column considers practical matters of timing and frequency. For this method, teams use established communication mechanisms if available, or they create their own. The team schedules some meetings regularly, schedules other meetings to coincide with project deliverables, and other meetings as needed. The team focuses on what stakeholders find helpful and not on what the team finds helpful. Just as the risk response matrix assigns risk ownership to a person, the team assigns one person to communicate with each stakeholder. To simplify communication, the team groups similar stakeholder requests

Table 6.3 Sample communication matrix

Stakeholder	Information on	Share	Timing/frequency	Method	Communication owner
Investor	Return on investment expectations	Project status and key issues	Kickoff meeting, then monthly	Conference calls and e-mail follow-up	Project manager
Developer	Construction plans and cost/benefit trade-offs	End-user needs and desires, costs	At the start and every 2 weeks	Conference calls and e-mail follow-up	Project manager
Construction company	Work progress and key issues	Construction plans	Every 2 weeks	On-site meetings	Construction site manager
Local government	Building rules and standards	Permits, requests, and construction plans	Initially, and then as needed	Department official forms	Developer
Customers	Needs and desires	Information	Initially, and upon project and building completion	Initial market analysis website, on-site inspections	Marketing agency

Adapted from Wells and Kloppenborg (2019, 49).

Table 6.4 Arboretum Agile project roadmap

Release 1	Release 2	Release 3	Release 4
Decision to apply	Prepare application	Install signs	High-resolution map
≥25 species	Support statements	Plan for more trees	Invasive removal
Trustee support	Create a basic map	Minimal tree trimming	More species planted
Tree committee support	Initial site preparation	Trustee tree planting	Donation requests

Adapted from Anantatmula and Kloppenborg (2021, 125–126).

together. The communication matrix defines stakeholder interactions and the dynamic Agile roadmap guides project work.

In the Agile approach, **information radiators** are tools that keep stakeholders informed. An example of an information radiator tool is the **Agile project roadmap**. Agile teams use this technique for initial planning and then adapt it as the project progresses. In the following example, one author led the project to create the product (an arboretum, i.e., a botanical garden for trees) (Table 6.4).

In Table 6.4, each column refers to a product release. In this example, spring and fall are the best seasons for planting, which determined the team's decision to use 6-month release cycles. Each column shows the planned deliverables for a release, with the most important ones listed first. The first project release proceeded as planned, but the later releases differed. Despite the changes, the overall project was a success.

The third visual tool used in the Agile approach is a Kanban board.

Figure 6.3 shows work planned ("to do"), "work in progress," and work completed and accepted ("done"). This communication tool lets team members and stakeholders follow the status of work products. Teams limit simultaneous tasks to focus on critical work, as depicted under "work in progress" with two work products.

Lead Communications for Leadership and Team Alignment

Teams want meetings and communication to be **productive**, and efficient and clear communication is key to collaboration, alignment, and dealing with uncertainty.

To Do		Work In Progress (2)	Done
Prepare application	Install signs	Trustee support	≥25 species
Prepare site	Trim trees	Decision to apply	Tree committee support
Create basic application	Trustees plant tree		
Write support statement	Create Plan for more trees		

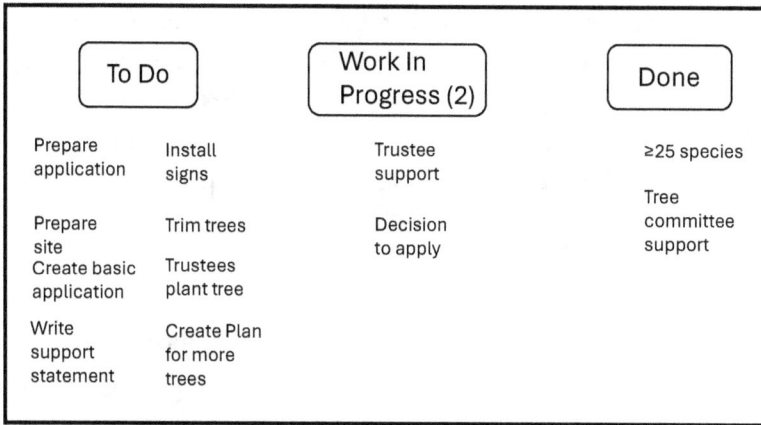

Figure 6.3 Kanban board example

We encourage you to:

- balance communication and share the right amount of information: clear, concise, and relevant;
- engage stakeholders and foster open discussions and a shared purpose to build trust and alignment; and
- leverage Agile tools and use visual aids like Kanban boards and roadmaps to keep teams informed and on track.

Clear and purposeful communication strengthens collaboration, keeps teams aligned, and ensures project success.

Run Productive Meetings

Agile projects use meetings for coordination, decisions, progress tracking, and problem-solving. However, meetings are time and people-intensive, which makes them costly. After discussing meetings, this section covers the Agile meeting cycle. Meetings need to be focused and result-oriented, avoiding unnecessary discussions or tangents.

Plan, Run, and Improve Meetings

Agile teams focus on efficiency, engagement, and continuous improvement. They follow these practices by holding **meetings** when necessary and keeping them time bound. For example, some meetings are short and involve a brief agenda and a handful of people. Other meetings are longer, with detailed agendas and more stakeholders. The advance distribution of the meeting agenda helps participants plan their workloads. Use meetings for essential topics, significant discussions/decisions, and other communication approaches if the purpose of the meeting is to share information.

Although the lead may change during the meeting depending on the topic, each lead keeps everyone engaged and uses the time productively. The team also tracks, assigns, and sets deadlines for actions. Agile teams track off-agenda topics in an issue log and address them later. If a meeting runs over schedule, the teams courteously ask participants if they can stay; otherwise, they reschedule the meeting. All meetings should end with the leader assessing successes, planning to repeat these practices, and noting areas for improvement.

Understand the Agile Meeting Cycle

The phrase "**Eat your dessert first**" mirrors the Agile principle of delivering what clients want as soon as possible. Agile meeting types have unique functions within the workflow:

1. backlog refinement
2. sprint planning
3. daily stand-up
4. sprint review
5. retrospective

To relate each meeting type to the Agile process, clients create an extensive wish list of items known as **user stories**. During backlog refinement meetings, the team prioritizes the most important tasks and the Product Owner clarifies these items to ensure developers understand their requirements.

A **sprint planning meeting** helps teams understand tasks before starting a sprint. The team and Product Owner agree on acceptance criteria to decide if the user story functions correctly and is acceptable. The Product

Owner proposes several user stories, and the team indicates how many they can develop in the upcoming cycle sprint. The process honors the stakeholder–team relationship because the Product Owner determines the priority, and the team decides on the work to do.

The third type of Agile meeting is the **daily stand-up**. These meetings are called stand-ups because they are short (typically 10 to 15 minutes) and focused. Each workday, teams meet quickly to discuss yesterday's work, today's plans, and potential problems. Participants receive updates but do not solve problems, as those discussions occur after the meeting between the two or three people who can address it.

The fourth type of Agile meeting is the **sprint review**. At this meeting, the client assesses the team's completed work against the agreed-upon standards of "done." Now that they have one use case story that works, clients will often state that their priorities have changed. This leads to the next backlog refinement meeting.

The last type of Agile meeting is a **retrospective**, which we discussed earlier. During the retrospective meeting, the team asks such questions as, what merits repetition, and what could improve with change? These focused discussions allow the teams to concentrate on customer-added value output.

Lead Meetings for Productivity and Impact

Teams want meetings and communication to be **productive and efficient**.

We encourage you to:

- **plan efficient meetings** with clear goals, concise agendas, and the right attendees;
- **focus meetings** by tracking decisions and actions and tabling unrelated topics; and
- **hold retrospective meetings** and reflect on what worked and what did not work to make meaningful adjustments.

Effective meetings lead to better teamwork and faster decisions.

Make Collaborative Decisions with Agile Practices

Effective decision making is critical to the success of Agile practices, and teams need to be fast, inclusive, adaptable, and focused on the project goals.

Ensure Decisions Are Timely and Practical

Agile projects call for many **decisions** from teams and stakeholders, where decisions involve a combination of judgment, facts, and instinct. Teams often select the best and most accepted decisions, but leaders keep some decision-making authority. Understanding when and how to decide is key to maintaining project momentum.

Align Decision Making with Agile Project Stages

Table 6.5 shows the timing of decisions over the project life cycle.

This list gives readers an idea of the wide range of decisions to be made.

Table 6.5 Types and timing of Agile project decisions

Before the project starts, select the	Early in the project, identify the	During the project, focus on	At the project conclusion, focus on
Project	Approach	Team development	Deliverables and customer readiness
Source	Success and trade-offs	Schedule	Team and rewards
Key personnel	Priorities	Quality	How to deliver continuous customer support
	Risks	Progress assessment	Ways to help team members in securing future work
	Commitment	Changes to accept	
	Team selection		

Strengthen Judgment for Effective Decisions

As individuals and groups work, the project **vision** is top of mind, guiding all decisions. The team prioritizes the project's needs over personal feelings toward team members. Facts are important for decision making, but sometimes intuition also plays a role. Inclusive and effective decisions result from teams that encourage open and honest dialogue.

Foster Collaborative Decision Making

Open communication leads to better decisions. Agile empowers those working most directly with stakeholders to make key decisions. This includes training the team to decide, share information, and gain support from senior leadership. The person with the final say evaluates every possibility and point of view. The quality of the decision hinges on both the decision maker and the method used.

Clarify Decision Ownership for Team Empowerment

Regarding **decision ownership**, various project decisions involve different individuals or groups. Sponsors or Product Owners make significant decisions and must be available. Product Owners conduct frequent daily meetings with teams to facilitate decisions. The Scrum Master empowers team members and minimizes intervening in team decision-making processes.

When leaders empower teams, they encourage discussions and recommendations to aid the formal leader's decision making. As applicable, other departments may be involved in making some decisions. One author collaborated with clients from two departments that had not worked well together. They assigned a representative from each department and tasked them with developing a joint recommendation.

Lead Agile Decision Making for Impact

Leaders who delegate **empower** their teams while ensuring alignment with broader strategic goals.

We encourage you to:

- **empower teams** by delegating decisions to those closest to the work,
- balance intuition and data when deciding, and
- **encourage open dialogue** to achieve well-informed decisions.

Collaborative decision making is key to the success of Agile practices because it empowers teams to make timely, inclusive choices that align with the project vision.

Build High-Performing Self-Managed Teams

Self-management is a key characteristic of Agile teams, and we equate high-performing teams with self-managed teams.

Understand Self-Managed Teams and Their Benefits

Self-managed teams reach a point where they require minimal direction. These long-lived teams stay together after completing a project and work on the next one together. The more they work and learn together, the more they achieve. These members understand the project vision and are accountable, respectful, and supportive. Self-managed teams offer several advantages, including increased autonomy, enhanced motivation, and improved innovation. Management empowers these teams to decide, solve problems, and take ownership of their work.

Stages of Team Development

Researchers have devoted significant attention to **team development** (Tuckman 1965; Highsmith 2009; Laloux 2014). Table 6.6 shows the Agile team development stages.

The first row shows how team members often feel at each stage, and the second row shows what team members do. The third row shows leadership strategies to help the team progress toward self-management.

Table 6.6 Agile team development stages

Stage of team development	Forming	Storming	Norming	Performing (self-managed)
Team member feels	Eager yet cautious	Resistant yet wishes to commit	Part of the team that will succeed	Close to team members and understand them
Team member does	Grasps expectations and organization	Jockeys for power; asks questions	Accepts team members, communicates openly	Improves self, expands leadership abilities beyond role
Project leader strategies	Develop the project charter and help members build relationships	Develop the team charter and define the processes	Focus on stakeholders and collaborate on decisions	Improve processes and communication, resolve conflicts
Helpful virtues	Imagination and foresight	Respect and trust	Expressiveness and commitment	Honesty and courage

Adapted from Kloppenborg and Petrick (1999); Kloppenborg et al. (2023, 161–162).

The last row shows some virtues to help move the team through the stages. To illustrate these phases, imagine a group of swimmers at a lake. In forming, they tentatively dipped their toes in the water to see how cold it was. In the storming stage, they jumped in and wondered if they had made the right decision. In the norming stage, they enjoyed the swim. Then, in the performing stage, they performed as if they were an Olympic synchronized swimming team.

Teams that experience disruption or change in membership may revert to an earlier stage of team development. Despite this, their overall progress will be positive. High-achieving teams also experience setbacks, but they rarely revert to the forming stage.

To explore each stage further, team members want to contribute in the **forming stage** but need guidance. They learn about the project, roles, the organization, and the decision-making processes. Until they get guidance, they question the project, the leadership, and their new teammates. These new team members often focus on self-development. Leaders guide them by describing the project vision and how the stakeholders will benefit.

These leaders also role model foresight as they get the team to help develop sections of the project charter. At first, leaders focus on team cohesion because when team members are unfamiliar with one another, power dynamics emerge and lead to tension, but over time, the tensions ease.

Project excitement boosts teamwork and, although initial project commitment by everyone is rare, it develops in the second or **storming stage**. In this stage, team members suggest different approaches to developing the project. If there is functional conflict, it offers value because it focuses on the work at hand. It is helpful when team members ask questions because ambiguity tolerances vary. Leaders help by outlining project plans and supporting team members to get to know each other to enhance their comfort of working together. Formal leaders encourage teams to develop a **team charter** to facilitate progress through the storming stage. Team charters include sections such as:

- responsibilities,
- respect,
- meeting conduct,
- decision making,
- reporting,
- conflict resolution, and
- continuous improvement.

Leaders build trust with a positive culture and logical processes. As members begin their work, leaders show trust and give them increasing latitude in deciding how to work. For instance, allowing the team to take part in creating the project charter shows respect.

As they work together, the team reaches the **norming stage**, where they embrace being part of a successful team. Members reach this point at their own pace. When teams are norming, members accept each other, including their idiosyncrasies. As team members develop trust with each other, they contribute with initial ideas on work products. As reflected in explicit and tacit ways (stated and unstated agreements), teams find their own ways of working beyond the team charter. Teamwork improves when leaders emphasize the project's goals and value. Team members develop commitment and support as leaders regularly communicate the project vision.

Table 6.7 Self-managed Agile team practices

Behavior	Communication methods	Project methods
Help others	Share information	Agree on goals
Be a team player	Value conflict of ideas	Plan collaboratively
Show mutual respect	Resolve interpersonal conflict	Use team charters
Focus on improvement	Surface problems	Hold each other accountable
Learn together	Tolerate minor mistakes	Solve problems together

Adapted from Kloppenborg et al. (2023, 162–166).

Some teams progress to a higher level, called **performing or self-managed**, which marks an exciting phase. Team members experience close friendships where the "tiger team" is excited, supportive, and trusting of each other. NASA popularized the term, notably during the Apollo 13 crisis. Agile and focused hunting makes the tiger the namesake of "tiger teams," so picture a team that tackles high-stakes problems. Table 6.7 lists some self-managed Agile team practices.

Based on one author's running experiences, here is an everyday example of how team members show leadership in their own way, learn from each other, and support each other.

We are runners (in our 50s, 60s, and 70s) and run together on Saturdays. As I grow older, my running declines slightly each year, so I seek ideas to slow that decline. Some runners (let's call them team members) lead by example. One runner takes quick, short steps, which running coaches often recommend for younger, competitive runners. Another keeps their shoulders straight and squared, as good posture helps one maintain pace. Meanwhile, another runner analyzed the sport and discovered that short walking breaks, particularly on hills, help a runner continue longer and achieve better training benefits. My spouse (who is also a runner) watches me with kindness and gently reminds me when I'm tired and not keeping my shoulders straight and squared. While not leaders, these teammates show leadership in their own way.

Outcomes and Advantages of Self-Managed Teams

Self-managed Agile teams deliver excellent project **results**. Throughout the project, they collaborate with stakeholders and meet and exceed stakeholder expectations. Project output helps stakeholders meet business needs and create value.

Besides stakeholder satisfaction, the parent organization, project team, and individual team members also benefit. The parent organization now has an effective team of committed and capable workers for future projects. The team members have an esprit de corps and are eager to work together again. The team is proud of its accomplishments and enjoys its work. Self-managed teams are a win for everyone.

Lead Self-Managed Teams Toward Collaboration and Excellence

The success of a project depends on strong decision making, leadership, and teamwork.

We encourage project leaders and team members to:

1. **empower the team**: Set clear expectations and allow team members to take ownership of their tasks. Support collaboration and reinforce shared accountability. Decide as close to the work as possible, empowering team members to act independently;
2. **build trust:** Communicate openly, resolve conflicts, and ensure everyone is accountable;
3. **lead your team through development:** Adapt your style as the team becomes more independent. Use strategies and virtues that help the team move through each stage of development; and
4. **foster team growth** through learning, idea sharing, and reflection.

Agile team leaders empower, trust, and guide their teams to collaborate and excel.

This chapter shows how Agile leadership empowers teams to own their work, adapt, and collaborate. Strong risk management, conflict resolution, and decision-making processes build resilience and alignment. Clear communication and structured meetings keep teams focused, while self-management drives motivation and innovation. These principles help leaders build high-performing teams. **In the VUCA world, these strategies cultivate a culture of trust, collaboration, and continuous improvement.**

Embrace the opportunity to put these principles into your leadership practice.

When leaders remove barriers and build trust, teams take ownership, solve problems, and drive success—step back, empower, and watch your teams rise to the challenge.

The next chapter examines ways to cultivate emergent leaders for the future.

Learn, Reflect, and Grow

Everyone has a unique way of learning and identifying areas for growth. As outlined at the end of Chapter 1, we encourage you to keep a journal. Improving skills is easier through experiential learning— "knowing, doing, and reflecting" (Kolb 2014). Review the following formats for ideas on journal topics:

- **What do I know?**
- **What am I doing?**
- **What am I reflecting on?**
- **What do we know?**
- **What are we doing?**
- **What are we reflecting on?**

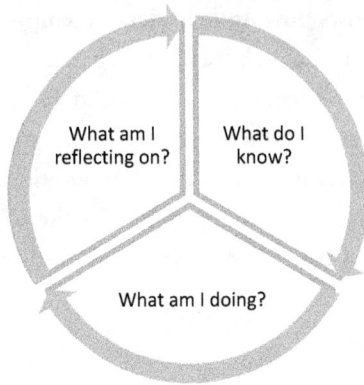

Figure 6.4 The experiential learning process (Kolb 2014)

This cycle is about improvement and change. It is a cycle of personal and team growth and development. Cultivating current and future leaders leaves a legacy of growth that continues to inspire and develop others. **Shared leadership is a collective responsibility.**

CHAPTER 7

Cultivate Emergent Leadership: Develop the Leaders of Tomorrow

We need to build more organizations that prioritize the care of human beings.

—Sinek (2014, 53)

Figure 7.1 shows that many of the actions leaders can take to cultivate leaders of tomorrow come from developmental leadership, and some come from Agile leadership.

Learning Goals

- **Describe** core principles of emergent leadership and their role in developing adaptable, self-directed leaders.
- **Identify** personal leadership strengths and growth areas through structured self-reflection.
- **Implement** strategies to build psychological safety and trust, fostering leadership development within a team.

Introduction

Earlier chapters present conceptual content on leadership. Chapter 2 explains leadership development virtues and behaviors in learning agility, trust, and hope. Dynamic environments call for flexible leadership styles to adapt to each situation. Chapter 3 details the importance of strong teams and positive working relationships for Agile leaders in meeting customer needs. By leading from behind (Chapter 4), they use developmental

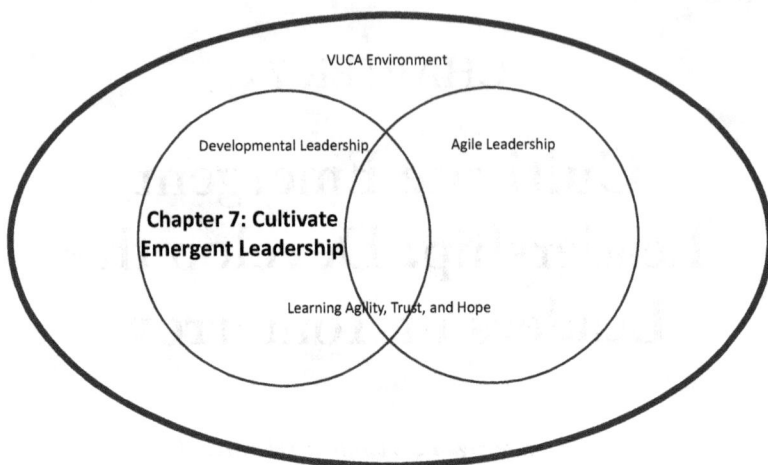

Figure 7.1 Developmental Agile Leadership roadmap

leadership to foster emergent leadership. Agile *and* developmental leadership involve shared leadership to create and support healthy workplaces.

Agile and developmental leaders are future and present focused, effective communicators, and problem solvers. Chapters 5 and 6 emphasize practical strategies leaders and teams can apply to build a strong, adaptive work culture. By integrating Agile techniques, structured decision making, and proactive problem-solving, these chapters provide actionable tools to develop resilient, high-performing teams.

In this chapter, we explore the concept of emergent leadership, focusing on developing tomorrow's leaders. The chapter develops empowering behind-the-scenes leaders. At the right time, leading from behind also involves helping individuals help each other lead.

The Essence of Emergent Leadership

Developing emergent leadership and growth involves establishing and maintaining open and authentic relationships. These relationships, built on mutual trust and respect, grow through genuine commitment. We are self-aware because we are conscious of our values and behaviors. However, it takes interactions with others to develop rapport and understand them before working well together. **A leader who leads from**

behind asks themselves, "How can I help my team members develop so they can help themselves, teammates, and stakeholders develop?"

Lead with Presence, Respect, and Authenticity

Leadership development requires presence, respect, and understanding of **diverse communication and learning styles.** Consider active listening and mindful presence to show commitment without judgment. Leadership development starts by assessing individual work styles and group interaction preferences. Appreciating different ways people express themselves and hone your abilities to work and communicate with others. Besides understanding communication and learning styles, it helps to discuss interests and build rapport. For example, Tim is an avid runner, and I was a runner for 30 years. In our initial discussions, we talked about running. As our familiarity with each other grew, I shared with him how much I missed being able to run. I enjoy "running" when I hear about the races he and his partner complete. Emergence on my part spanned a few years, as I learned how to lead while writing this applied book with Tim's guidance and coaching.

Key Principles of Emergent Leadership

To develop emergent leadership in your team, begin by covering concepts on Developmental Agile Leadership. **Set the stage** with your role as a Developmental Agile Leader who offers a supportive, behind-the-scenes presence. Recall that this form of leadership is about supporting followers and stakeholders from behind. Agile methodologies involve shared leadership and work in dynamic environments with their teams. **Remind emergent leaders that presence from behind does not signify absence.**

To draw from specific chapters, consider discussing the value of emergent leadership development for the changing workplace (VUCA world—Chapter 1). Then, introduce leadership values and virtues such as learning agility, trust, hope, ethical conduct, and humility (Chapter 2). Chapter 2 shows that learning agility, trust, and hope help develop Agile leadership. Based on Chapters 3 and 4, discuss the role of learning agility in developing leadership.

As the discussions turned to putting Developmental Agile Leadership into practice for the emergent leader to try, focus on the material in Chapters 5 to 7. Chapter 5 introduces the concept that leaders and teams cultivate a growth mindset culture by learning, adapting, and solving problems together through trust, communication, and Agile techniques. Future leaders will gain skills in teamwork, adaptability, and problem-solving. Chapter 6 shows how Agile leaders help teams and stakeholders own their work, handle problems, and work together. Emerging leaders build high-performing teams by mastering risk management, conflict resolution, and communication. Throughout, share your feelings and struggles in past decision-making situations.

Share Leadership Journeys and Insights to Inspire Growth

Genuine leaders care for and value each person as an individual. They establish relationships and focus on individual needs. The aim is to identify and encourage those who can lead by leading informally on topics within their sphere of knowledge. As mentees hear from others about their career progression, they can reflect on personal strengths, interests, and aspirations. To exemplify some scenarios:

- Some may express a desire to remain a team member and develop additional technical skills. Here, you can emphasize that technical expertise and leadership skills are not mutually exclusive. You can highlight the importance of understanding strengths and weaknesses before applying for a promotion.
- Others may say they are comfortable with technical roles and reluctant to lead. Here, you can share an example of the fear of failing or an instance of failure and what you learned. This may lead to a conversation on the benefits of failing and valuing psychological safety.
- Some team members may state that they aspire to be project managers. Here, you could discuss the merits of shadowing a team lead and project manager and networking with a few people to learn about their career progression. This helps team members understand training and experience gaps.

- In situations where heavy workloads hinder leadership development, you can discuss self-directed learning opportunities.

Early discussions with emerging leaders reveal leadership development needs and help identify shadowing and networking opportunities.

Lay the Foundations for Emergent Leadership

Emergent leadership thrives when individuals sense value, support, and empowerment. Build relationships to help others grow and learn; align personal strengths with collective goals and reinforce key leadership values.

We encourage leaders and emergent leaders to:

- **form strong bonds** with mentees by learning about their goals, abilities, and obstacles;
- **discuss the nature of leadership** in a VUCA world, emphasizing adaptability, learning agility, trust, and hope;
- **demonstrate presence and respect** with active listening, constructive feedback, and consistent support; and
- **help team members** reflect on their strengths, values, and leadership to set development goals.

To encourage leaders to emerge, create a culture of trust, reflection, and growth.

The Role of Reflection in Leadership Growth

Leaders and followers who reflect together grow stronger. Begin by exploring how leadership development provides purpose and meaning in work. Journaling reflections help clarify thoughts and track progress.

Develop Self-Awareness for More Decisive Leadership

Self-awareness and reflection are essential for developing leadership skills. Self-awareness involves understanding strengths and abilities (competencies) and identifying areas for growth and development. To develop self-awareness, stay open-minded and question your ideas and opinions. Sometimes, ideas are based on an incomplete understanding or biases. As we develop self-awareness, we improve our ability to relate to others and connect with them.

Leaders can ask followers self-reflection questions such as, *What went well today? Where can I improve?* and *What patterns do I notice in my reactions?* These types of questions help identify habits, stress triggers, as well as rewarding aspects of work.

Help Team Members Build Confidence

Building **confidence** involves supporting people's growth by providing resources and a healthy environment. Encourage reluctant followers by highlighting their past achievements. Established leaders offer support to those followers needing guidance to step up. A supportive environment includes praise, constructive criticism, open discussions about psychological safety, and learning from mistakes.

Foster Psychological Safety and Trust

Everyone has a different level of comfort for change or trying something new. **Psychological safety** is the "perception of the consequences of taking interpersonal risks, most notably at work" (Edmondson and Bransby 2023, 56). When individuals experience psychological safety, it can enhance trust, cooperation, problem-solving, and knowledge sharing. Psychological safety helps us develop as resilient and curious leaders.

Lead with Curiosity, Courage, and Adaptability

Curious leaders understand and practice psychological safety; they recognize that failure is sometimes inevitable and that when they fail, they will embrace it. Curious leaders do not focus on perfectionism or dwell on their mistakes; they are open-minded and interested in ideas and practice. **Courage** involves bravery in taking a calculated risk and acting in situations where fear may or may not be involved. Sometimes, it can be a brave act to try something different. Help new leaders gain confidence by encouraging incremental innovative idea development and experimentation.

Related to psychological safety, there may be an opportunity to discuss **self-compassion**, a subset of compassion. Compassion means being kind, understanding, and sympathetic toward others. Note that self-worth and well-being relate to self-compassion. Practicing self-compassion helps us understand everyone makes mistakes. The past is the past, and dwelling on the past is unhelpful. In developing self-compassion, we develop compassion for others. Compassion also fosters a **growth mindset.** When we have a willingness to learn, we can cope with change.

Use Reflection to Develop New Leaders

As leaders, we encourage you to guide team members in **self-reflection** by explaining its value and providing practical ways to start. Ask how you can aid their safety and confidence, then act, showing self-compassion and encouraging them to do so too.

We encourage leaders and emergent leaders to:

- **reflect on personal growth** by identifying strengths, challenges, and improvement areas,
- **create a safe space** where team members can share ideas and take risks without fear,
- **stay open-minded** by embracing new ideas and learning from mistakes, and
- **remain kind to yourself** by viewing setbacks as learning opportunities.

Leadership development is an ongoing journey of growth, reflection, and practice—by setting clear goals, embracing challenges, and fostering accountability, leaders and emerging leaders strengthen their skills and create lasting impact.

Practical Strategies for Leadership Development

As you focus on practical **strategies**, remember that leadership needs change, so expect shifts in skills, goals, and areas for improvement. New leaders often arise when members see a need and step up, or when others recognize their potential. Regular discussions and maintaining journals are helpful because they foster reflection. Throughout, it helps to consider the alignment between values and behaviors. Personal growth is important for everyone, from entry-level employees to the CEO. Agile projects and, indeed, all organizations want workers who are:

- self-motivated,
- creative,
- able to influence others,
- self-managers,
- adaptable, and
- team oriented.

Design and Implement a Leadership Growth Plan

A **leadership growth plan** involves establishing achievable, incremental objectives suitable for individual skills. This approach manages expectations and fosters incremental development. While achieving these goals is rewarding and can spur progress, it is as important to learn from failures. After establishing the plan, concentrate on finding appropriate leadership training. Jointly establish SMART goals—Specific, Measurable, Achievable, Realistic, and Time bound. Develop a strategy to help the individual progress and remember that stretch goals are fine, but overly complex goals are not. You want members to be inspired and see progress, but you do not want them to be disheartened by unrealistic goals.

From the leader's perspective, a key task is aligning mentorship objectives with individual aspirations. This alignment is essential for mentorship. Mentoring many individuals presents challenges for leaders with limited time. To help with training, the team leader can draw from the concept of a **community of practice** and schedule lunch-and-learns. These sessions can help balance workloads for mentoring multiple emerging leaders.

Everyone's emergent leadership strategy will be unique. As the leadership journey unfolds, revisit the leadership plan to ensure that the plan remains relevant and practical. Over time, consider repeating the above exercise with midterm goals to keep the plan dynamic and responsive to changing needs. Leadership development is based on collaboration and support from a trusted adviser.

Create Developmental Opportunities for Developing Leaders

With a personal development plan in place, the leader seeks **opportunities** for the member to experiment with leadership activities. Followers learn leadership by doing and then discussing what they learned. Strive to match tasks to individuals but let them figure out how to do the activity if there is no established method.

Apply the "**One Push**" rule when offering development opportunities. Provide employees with challenges that push them slightly out of their comfort zone and avoid overwhelming them. Assign manageable tasks, assess performance, and ensure challenge levels are right—not too much, but enough to foster growth. This is like the Goldilocks approach from Chapter 6, which aligns well with incremental growth and avoids the risks of stress and disengagement.

Encourage Accountability, Commitment, and Continuous Improvement

The leader and team member develop a brief **accountability agreement** outlining their work relationship and commitments. For example, the accountability agreement could cover such topics as: who are:

- confidentiality, respect, and professional conduct;
- ethics in leadership, continuous learning, and a growth mindset;
- joint accountability regarding taking responsibility and following through.

As a PhD student, one author established an accountability agreement with their adviser to exemplify an accountability agreement. Every

Wednesday morning by 7 a.m., the student submitted their work, and the adviser provided feedback within 48 hours. The structure promoted steady progress and urgency, even resulting in late-night work on Tuesdays. The student completed the dissertation well ahead of most durations for a doctorate.

Practice and Role-Play

Before trying a developmental leadership activity, consider **role-playing** and **what-if scenarios**. These strategies offer a safe environment to ask questions, discuss concerns, and practice. After a leadership development activity, leaders and followers discuss the experience and leadership skills used, and assess growth. Then, the two can role-play a new exercise before the next leadership activity.

Use Leadership Journaling as a Growth Tool

The leader and follower can maintain reflective **journals** online or in hard copies. They can keep journals for personal use, and share ideas when ready. Journaling helps because it boosts creativity, critical thinking, and self-improvement. Suggested topics to prompt journaling follow:

- What is my perspective on assuming a leadership role?
- What motivates my leadership ambitions?
- What excites me about becoming a leader?
- What are my concerns about becoming a leader?
- What is one short-term developmental leadership goal, and what else connects to it?
- What do I do well? What is an area for growth? What do I need to learn? How do I proceed?

Analyzing an activity involves noting its challenges, comfort level, and unexpected elements. Although conducted in hindsight, consider a pre-mortem before starting a developmental leadership task and then evaluate progress during and following the task. These activities help with self-development from opinions toward self-realization.

Apply Practical Guidelines for Leadership Growth

Leadership development is a joint journey of self-discovery and co-discovery.

We encourage leaders and emergent leaders to:

- **set SMART goals** for leadership development and track progress through small, manageable challenges;
- **use the "One Push"** rule of thumb when giving development tasks and motivate employee development without excessive pressure;
- **keep a reflective journal** to explore motivations, concerns, and areas for growth as leaders; and
- **create an accountability agreement** to clarify expectations and improve commitment and trust.

Ongoing growth involves goal-setting, embracing challenges, and self-reflection.

Support the Next Generation of Leaders

Leaders empower others by collaborating and supporting them once they establish a supportive environment.

Understand and Adapt to the Needs of Emerging Leaders

To develop effective leadership, leaders offer different levels of support based on individual needs. A leader who promotes growth and development stays engaged and supportive with:

- encouragement and support to take calculated risks that push individuals beyond their comfort zones;
- recognition and celebrations of achievements to build confidence;
- tailored feedback, support through growing pains, and coaching during resistance to change;

- leadership developmental goals aligned with organizational objectives;
- assessments of decision-making abilities and confidence to foster growth;
- help with emotional and psychological barriers to success;
- being present and supportive in career development, including networking opportunities; and
- encouragement for self-reflective and self-discovery exercises.

Leaders and team members meet often to review progress, discuss problems, and plan for future development. These practices help leaders and individuals see when an emerging leader is ready to mentor others.

Be a Mentor and Champion for Future Leaders

Emerging leaders gain confidence as they learn and grow their leadership skills, and over time, **the mentee will be ready to mentor others.** Leaders guide people using developmental, emergent leadership when they:

- share their leadership journey to help new leaders understand their struggles and successes;
- share leadership roles and responsibilities;
- model coaching and mentoring, as well as self-reflection and awareness; and
- celebrate successes and stay present throughout the journey.

The leader fosters a supportive team environment that helps everyone grow and develop. Imagine **a not-too-distant future where several leaders guide multiple emerging leaders.** Each leader shares roles and responsibilities with their mentees and, in due course, the number of leaders increases! This approach fosters a more dynamic—and, dare we say, stronger—ecosystem that continues to grow.

Take Meaningful Action to Develop Future Leaders

Leaders support their mentees' growth through regular discussions and consistent presence. Leaders help the mentees determine when they are ready to mentor others.

We encourage leaders and emergent leaders to:

- **empower your team** and make expectations clear and let them take charge of their tasks. Support collaborations and reinforce shared accountability. Make informed decisions at the lowest possible level, closest to the customer; and
- **help teams grow** by encouraging learning, sharing ideas, and reflecting on experiences.

In conclusion, developing emergent leaders is a dynamic process. Leaders create a learning environment by empowering individuals from behind. Mentorship and self-reflection help create successful, collaborative teams by building confident, inspiring leaders. *Embrace the leadership journey with courage and curiosity—your growth and those you lead depend on it.*

Embrace the opportunity to put these principles into your leadership practice.

The best leaders do not just lead—they create the conditions for leadership to emerge in others—who will you empower to step forward next?

As we approach the final chapter, we share concluding thoughts and offer hopes for continuing your leadership journey.

Learn, Reflect, and Grow

Everyone has a unique way of learning and identifying areas for growth. As outlined at the end of Chapter 1, we encourage you to keep a journal. Improving skills is easier through experiential learning—"knowing, doing, and reflecting," (Kolb 2014). Review the following formats for ideas on journal topics:

- What do I know?
- What am I doing?
- What am I reflecting on?

- What do we know?
- What are we doing?
- What are we reflecting on?

This cycle is about improvement and change (Figure 7.2). It is a cycle of personal and team growth and development. Cultivating current and future leaders leaves a legacy of growth that continues to inspire and develop others. **Shared leadership is a collective responsibility.**

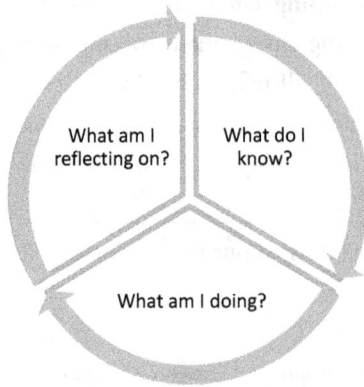

Figure 7.2 The experiential learning process (Kolb 2014)

CHAPTER 8

Developmental Agile Leadership: Bringing It All Together

In Agile environments, leaders empower teams by fostering a culture of learning and development, not with control. And in doing so trust and collaboration drive success and innovation (Sutherland and Sutherland 2015).

Developmental leadership + Agile = Developmental Agile Leadership

Figure 8.1 summarizes this book, showing how both developmental and Agile leadership overlap and work in parallel to guide leaders' beliefs and actions in our turbulent times.

Learning Goals

- **Adopt** the mindset of a Developmental Agile Leader to guide your actions and inspire others.
- **Turn** obstacles into growth opportunities by applying Agile principles and leadership skills in dynamic environments.
- **Nurture** a culture of trust, adaptability, and resilience within your team, empowering them to thrive in uncertainty.
- **Lead** with vision and purpose, motivating others to realize their full potential while navigating complexity.
- **Reflect** on your leadership journey and dedicate yourself to continuous growth, embodying Developmental Agile Leadership.

Figure 8.1 Developmental Agile Leadership roadmap

Thrive in a VUCA World

We wrote this book in the fast-paced, ever-changing twenty-first century, aware that challenges and difficulties are unavoidable. Simple solutions are seldom sufficient, and uncertainty is a constant. Yet, as we have explored, the VUCA world presents risks and opportunities.

This chapter highlights how developmental leadership and Agile leadership enhance individual and team performance.

Understand VUCA Challenges

We use the acronym **VUCA** to describe the uncertain landscape. Separately, each element may call for a different type of decision:

- **Volatility**: Make quick decisions to respond to rapid changes.
- **Uncertainty**: Use more information to decide.
- **Complexity**: Reflect, reframe, and focus on one part of the issue at a time.
- **Ambiguity**: Experiment to understand the situation before deciding.

Organizations face various combinations of VUCA, making decision making complex and flexible leadership styles proves beneficial.

Adapt Leadership Styles for VUCA Environments

Earlier chapters explore three distinct *leadership styles* for a turbulent environment. Each style offers advantages, and leaders adapt their approach to fit the team's and stakeholders' needs.

- **Transformational leaders** lead from the top (or front) and are visionary; they inspire significant changes.
- **Servant leaders** lead from the middle, work with their teams, and empower them to solve problems quickly, as seen in the Agile approach.
- **Developmental leaders**, also known as emergent leaders, lead from behind. They help members cocreate leadership plans and develop into leaders. We describe this style as informal leadership.

Agile leadership combines all three styles (leading from the front, middle, and back).

Integrate Development and Agile into a Unified Leadership Strategy

Throughout this book, we discuss how **developmental leadership and Agile leadership** inspire better leadership and empower emergent leaders and teams. Together, these approaches focus on skill-building and positive values. The connections between these leadership approaches are strong and impactful.

Now, it is your turn to take these concepts and turn them into actionable steps to help you, your teams, and your customers thrive in the changing world.

This book explores three elements of Developmental Agile Leadership:

1. **Principles**: Create a stakeholder-centered culture emphasizing learning agility, trust, and hope.
2. **Mindset**: Foster continuous learning through reflection and feedback.

3. **Developmental Agile Leadership:** Apply these principles and mindset to empower individuals, cultivate leadership, and strengthen teams.

Lead with values, think and act with agility, and prioritize collaboration.

Leadership is about helping others grow—when you share, support, and adapt, you build stronger teams and future leaders.

Principles: Build a Stakeholder-Focused Culture Emphasizing Learning Agility, Trust, and Hope

Starting with the first element on **principles**, earlier chapters cover respecting everyone to foster a strong learning culture where valued members and stakeholders reciprocate. Teamwork also helps project leaders prioritize stakeholder needs. Learning agility drives the culture when leaders:

- lead with courage by fostering a stakeholder-focused culture;
- advocate for the team and its success;
- encourage reciprocity when team members and stakeholders show trust or learning agility; and
- align words and actions, especially in a crisis.

Cultivate a Stakeholder-Focused Culture

Leaders in a **culture** focused on stakeholders emphasize customer value as the team's top priority. The team defines success from the customer's point of view and works to deliver value. Project leaders share the stakeholder vision of the project with the team to guide them and help them progress. Throughout, they give the team frequent feedback on progress.

Project leaders respect stakeholder rights and responsibilities and encourage the team to do the same. Stakeholders provide timely decisions to maintain project momentum as the team creates value-adding work products for them. Throughout, leaders ensure the project is well-supported and visible.

Build Trust Within Teams

Project leaders also **care** about the well-being of team members and stakeholders. They recognize that **trust** is essential for success—without it, nothing else matters. Leaders create a supportive environment where everyone can share ideas and try new things. Leaders are consistent in words and actions; they keep their promises and show integrity. As a result, everyone works in a project environment reflecting:

- honesty and respect;
- collaboration and a willingness to share ideas;
- open communication, including during hard conversations;
- psychological safety and freedom to ask questions;
- safe space for risk-taking; and
- a bias for action.

Project leaders avoid conflicts of interest to build trust; trust is fragile, and it erodes when collaborators suspect hidden agendas or favoritism. These leaders acknowledge their mistakes, take responsibility, and work to prevent similar issues in the future.

Foster Hope in Leadership

When team members and stakeholders have **hope**, they believe the project they are working on will create useful solutions. This enhances their motivation and perseverance. The team cultivates resilience by recognizing that success is attainable, even when they face obstacles and setbacks.

Leaders build collective hope and unity by sharing clear goals and encouraging collaborations. Leaders seek help when needed and encourage others to do the same. Project leaders foster resilience by helping teams overcome challenges and focus on solutions. They ask what they can do to help boost their confidence, and then they follow through with help.

Develop Learning Agility

In uncertain and chaotic times, project teams and organizations capable of rapidly **learning together** gain a notable advantage over those that resist change. Agile leaders consider all viewpoints to foster positive dialogue. They keep the project vision, facts, and sound judgment at the forefront of decision-making processes. They evaluate work, assess the results, and act on what they learn to improve customer solutions. They make prompt decisions by using all relevant information to ensure project continuity. Learning-agile individuals continue to learn and improve.

Strengthen trust, hope, and learning agility in practice

To foster the **principles** of trust, hope, and learning agility as you lead:

- act courageously to inspire trust, hope, and learning among team members and stakeholders;
- focus on customer value to guide the project vision;
- create a consistent, safe, and open environment to build trust;
- build collective hope to help the team develop resilience to overcome setbacks so that they succeed; and
- recognize that when teams listen to each other and experiment on work products together, they learn swiftly together.

Stay true to your principles.

Remain optimistic, and trust yourself and your team members.

Mindset: Foster Continuous Learning Through Reflection and Feedback

Actively Seek and Embrace Feedback

Turning to the second principle on **mindset**, project leaders emphasize the merits of seeking feedback and encouraging their team to do the same because they understand the importance of open communication to keep everyone updated and foster collaboration. Agile leaders use roadmaps and Kanban boards to communicate progress and place them where stakeholders can follow developments.

Respond to Feedback

Sharing information helps teams work faster and make better decisions. Teams engage with feedback through active listening and a readiness to accept potential changes. Agile teams that perform well value feedback, collaborate, and deliver better customer value. These teams also adapt their practices to changing stakeholder needs.

Reflect on the Leadership Journey

Project leaders guide every team member and stakeholder in leadership development. They consider the perspectives of the individuals and groups they are helping and strive to understand and treat each person as an individual with unique strengths and desires. These leaders encourage self-**reflection** in leadership development. Project leaders model the behaviors they want their team members and stakeholders to emulate. Some of these key behaviors include:

- humility,
- relationship building,
- active listening,
- self-compassion, and
- sharing credit.

Encourage Rapid Learning and Growth

Project leaders promote **learning, experimentation, and continuous improvement.** They often use a plan–do–check–act approach to get teams and stakeholders to work together. Step-by-step, they motivate individuals to move out of their comfort zone and try new leadership activities. They reframe failure as a learning opportunity by emphasizing lessons learned rather than mistakes.

Strategies to accelerate learning

To foster the **mindset** of learning for individuals and teams through reflection and feedback as you lead:

- embrace feedback and listen with openness to the views of others;
- listen to understand and then respond thoughtfully and without delay;
- collaborate with each person and team on the leadership development journey to foster partnerships; and
- encourage learning, experimentation, and a culture of continuous growth.

Leadership is about developing others.

Lead with openness and curiosity.

Understand that each moment of feedback and collaboration deepens learning and nurtures growth in those you lead and yourself.

Developmental Agile Leadership: Empower Individuals to Grow and Strengthen Team Leadership

Developmental Agile Leadership is the application of these principles and mindset to empower individuals, cultivate leadership, and strengthen teams. Project leaders enhance customer value by developing people and teams when they:

- cocreate leadership development plans for individuals and groups;
- promote shared decision making;
- consider challenges and setbacks as opportunities for growth; and
- motivate teams to become self-managed teams.

Create Personalized Leadership Development Plans

Project leaders aim to empower individuals, teams, and stakeholders. They seek to lead and develop self-managed individuals, teams, and stakeholders. They start by forming strong relationships and they show presence for each person's needs and respect and understanding. Initial conversations cover the changing workplace, learning agility, trust, and hope. They work together to create a **leadership plan** that blends personal goals with company aims. They develop a unique leadership plan for each individual and team that includes SMART goals. This approach is not prescriptive, as some leaders experiment with coaching and empowerment to see what works best for follower development, but other leaders may start with training opportunities.

Gradually Share Decision Making

Leaders give teams increased **responsibilities** as they exhibit effective decision-making skills. By using data, feedback, and a variety of perspectives, teams work through problems in stages. The process is about sharing leadership as teams and individuals earn trust. For example, a motivated team will often be more successful in implementing a decision they made than a better decision given to them. As project leaders share decision making, they:

- empower others by helping them make decisions so they, too, contribute to a culture of trust;
- build trust by delegating tasks as teams and individuals show they can handle them;
- recognize that unfavorable choices provide valuable lessons and are starting points for growth; and
- have decisions made at the level closest to the customer whenever practical.

Reframe Challenges as Opportunities for Development

Project leaders customize development plans for individuals and teams by **matching** personal goals to project needs and organizational goals.

Leaders also give others the chance to lead and develop their skills. They turn challenges into opportunities for learning and innovation. Leaders push their teams to grow by tackling challenging situations and reflecting on their learning.

Project leaders help teams identify and prioritize risks and conflicts, and then the team decides which risks and conflicts to address and which to manage reactively. The team chooses the best risk response strategy for every situation and conflict.

Encourage Self-Management Within Teams

Self-managing teams are ideal for leaders who value collaboration and learning from challenges. As teams make more decisions, project leaders have more time to focus on strategic issues. Self-managing team members gain more control over their destinies and often experience greater satisfaction. These teams also achieve superior project results, resulting in happy clients. Self-managed teams keep each other accountable and celebrate their achievements.

Strategies to empower individuals and teams to reach their goals

---

To foster **Developmental Agile Leadership** and empower individuals and teams to reach their goals as you lead:

- cocreate a unique development plan with and for each individual and team;
- share decision making as teams and individuals learn to make effective choices;
- reframe risks, conflicts, and other challenges as opportunities for development; and
- assist your team in progressing toward self-management.

Lead with purpose and intention.

Know that by empowering individuals and fostering their growth, you not only help them reach their goals but also build *a resilient, Agile team that thrives in any environment.*

Final Thoughts and Hopes

In Chapter 1, we began by discussing the challenges of the unpredictable world. We emphasized leadership rooted in adaptability and agility. Then, in Chapter 2, we discussed the importance of learning agility, trust, and hope in building resilience. In Chapters 3 and 4, we focused on Agile and developmental leadership. Agile leaders make quick decisions and communicate openly. A developmental leader steps back to let their team take charge. Both types of leadership emphasize empowering others and sharing roles and responsibilities. In the subsequent chapters, we examined how these leadership styles create better workplaces. We explored emerging leadership concepts designed to help individuals become leaders. Nurturing current and future leaders establishes a legacy of growth that continues to inspire and develop others. In this way, shared leadership promotes collective responsibility.

We hope this book empowers you to navigate a complex world with resilience. We hope you use the ideas in this book to enhance your leadership and help others reach their potential. We hope you also embrace leading from various positions in your organization. We hope you stay dedicated to your leadership development and that of your team members and stakeholders. *Trust your judgment and build upon the insights from this book to guide you on your journey.*

Lead with the principles and mindset of Developmental Agile Leadership:

> *Leadership is more than what you do—it is about how you inspire and support others to be the best leaders they can be.*

> *Developmental Agile Leadership is one of continuous growth.*

> *Embrace the journey with courage and curiosity—your growth and the growth of those you lead depend on it.*

Learn, Reflect, and Grow

Everyone has a unique way of learning and identifying areas for growth. As outlined at the end of Chapter 1, we encourage you to keep a journal. Improving skills is easier through experiential learning— **"knowing, doing, and reflecting"** (Kolb 2014). Review the following formats for ideas on journal topics:

- **What do I know** now about my leadership strengths and areas for growth?
- **What am I doing** to apply Developmental Agile Leadership principles in my daily interactions?
- **What am I reflecting on** from my leadership experiences, and how will it shape my approach?
- **What do we know** about leadership, trust, and collaboration as a team?
- **What are we doing** to strengthen our leadership practices and team dynamics?
- **What are we reflecting on** as a team, and how will it inform our next steps?

This cycle is about improvement and change (Figure 8.2). It is a cycle of personal and team growth and development. Cultivating current and future leaders leaves a legacy of growth that continues to inspire and develop others. **Shared leadership is a collective responsibility.**

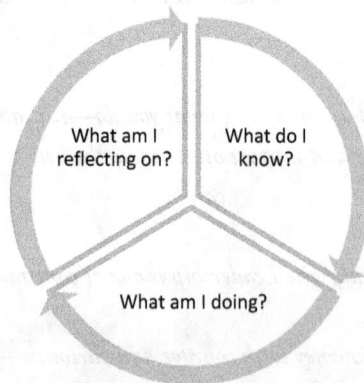

Figure 8.2 The experiential learning process (Kolb 2014)

References

Anantatmula, Vittal, and Timothy J. Kloppenborg. 2021. *Be Agile, Do Agile: Portfolio and Project Management*. Business Expert Press.

Aristotle. 1984. *The Complete Works of Aristotle: The Revised Oxford Translation*, edited by Jonathan Barnes. Princeton University Press.

Beck, Kent, Mike Beedle, Arie van Bennekum, et al. 2001. "Manifesto for Agile Software Development." *Agile Alliance*. https://agilemanifesto.org/.

Bennett, Nathan, and G. James Lemoine. 2014. "What a Difference a Word Makes: Understanding Threats to Performance in a VUCA World." *Business Horizons* 57 (3): 311–17. https://doi.org/10.1016/j.bushor.2014.01.001.

Bligh, Michelle C. 2017. "Leadership and Trust." In *Leadership Today: Practices for Personal and Professional Performance*, edited by Joan Marques and Satinder Dhiman. Springer.

Bragger, Jennifer D., Nicole A. Alonso, Kayla D'Ambrosio, and Nikita Williams. 2021. "Developing Leaders to Serve and Servants to Lead." *Human Resource Development Review* 20 (1): 9–45. https://doi.org/10.1177/1534484320981198.

Burke, C. Shawn, Dana E. Sims, Elizabeth H. Lazzara, and Eduardo Salas. 2007. "Trust in Leadership: A Multi-Level Review and Integration." *The Leadership Quarterly* 18 (6): 606–32. https://doi.org/10.1016/j.leaqua.2007.09.006.

Cerff, Karen, and Bruce E. Winston. 2006. "The Inclusion of Hope in the Servant Leadership Model." *Servant Leadership Research Roundtable*. Accessed February 12, 2025. https://web.archive.org/web/20180512081422id_/https://www.regent.edu/acad/global/publications/sl_proceedings/2006/cerff_winston.pdf.

Church, Allan H., and Gina A. Seaton. 2022. "Learning Agility as a Key Driver of Leadership Potential for Talent Identification, Pipeline Development, and Succession Planning in Organizations." *Consulting Psychology Journal: Practice and Research* 74 (3): 237–52. https://doi.org/10.1037/cpb0000238.

Cockburn, Alistair. n.d. "Agile Is an Attitude, Not a Technique with Boundaries. An Attitude Has No Boundaries, So We Wouldn't Ask 'Can I Use Agile Here,' But Rather 'How Would I Act in the Agile Way Here?' or 'How Agile Can We Be, Here?'" Accessed March 1, 2025. https://www.azquotes.com/quote/1246669.

Colla, Rachel, Paige Williams, Lindsay G. Oades, and Jesus Camacho-Morles. 2022. "'A New Hope' for Positive Psychology: A Dynamic Systems Reconceptualization of Hope Theory." *Frontiers in Psychology* 13:809053. https://doi.org/10.3389/fpsyg.2022.809053.

Covey, Stephen R., A. Roger Merrill, and Rebecca R. Merrill. 1995. *First Things First*. Simon and Schuster.

De Meuse, Kenneth P. 2017. "Learning Agility: Its Evolution as a Psychological Construct and Its Empirical Relationship to Leader Success." *Consulting Psychology Journal: Practice and Research* 69 (4): 267–95. https://doi.org/10.1037/cpb0000100.

De Meuse, Kenneth P., Guangrong Dai, George S. Hallenbeck, and King Yii Tang. 2008. "Using Learning Agility to Identify High Potentials Around the World." *Korn/Ferry Institute*. Accessed February 12, 2025. https://www.acumen.org.nz/uploads/3/8/1/3/38130931/whitepaperlearning_agility_research_10-10-2008.pdf.

Deming, W. Edwards. 1986. *Out of the Crisis*. MIT Press.

Dirks, Kurt T., and Daniel P. Skarlicki. 2007. "Trust in Leaders: Existing Research and Emerging Issues." In *Trust and Distrust in Organizations: Dilemmas and Approaches*, edited by Roderick M. Kramer and Karen S. Cook. Russell Sage Foundation.

Drucker, Peter. 1993. *Post-Capitalist Society*. HarperBusiness.

Dweck, Carol S. 1986. "Motivational processes affecting learning." *American Psychologist* 41 (10): 1040–48. https://doi.org/10.1037/0003-066X.41.10.1040.

Dweck, Carol S. 2009. "Developing Talent Through a Growth Mindset." *Olympic Coach* 21 (1): 4–7. https://www.growthmindsetinstitute.org/wp-content/uploads/2018/07/OlympCoachMag_Win-09_Vol-21_Mindset_Carol-Dweck-6.pdf.

Edmondson, A. C., and D. P. Bransby. 2023. "Psychological Safety Comes of Age: Observed Themes in an Established Literature." *Annual Review of Organizational Psychology and Organizational Behavior* 10 (1): 55–78. https://doi.org/10.1146/annurev-orgpsych-120920-055217.

Edmondson, Amy C. 2019. *The Fearless Organization: Creating Psychological Safety in the Workplace for Learning, Innovation, and Growth*. Wiley.

Edmondson, Amy C. 2023. *Right Kind of Wrong: Why Learning to Fail Can Teach Us to Thrive*. Random House.

Ely, Katherine, Lisa A. Boyce, Johnathan K. Nelson, Stephen J. Zaccaro, Gina Hernez-Broome, and Wynne Whyman. 2010. "Evaluating Leadership Coaching: A Review and Integrated Framework." *The Leadership Quarterly* 21 (4): 585–99. https://doi.org/10.1016/j.leaqua.2010.06.003.

George, Bill. 2010. *True North: Discover Your Authentic Leadership*. Vol. 143. John Wiley & Sons.

Gilley, Jerry W., Paul M. Shelton, and Ann Gilley. 2011. "Developmental Leadership: A New Perspective for Human Resource Development." *Advances in Developing Human Resources* 13 (3): 386–405. https://doi.org/10.1177/1523422311424264.

Greenleaf, Robert K. 1998. *The Power of Servant Leadership*. Berrett-Koehler Publishers.

Hannah, Sean T., Mary Uhl-Bien, Bruce J. Avolio, and Fabrice L. Cavarretta. 2009. "A Framework for Examining Leadership in Extreme Contexts." *The Leadership Quarterly* 20 (6): 897–919. https://doi.org/10.1016/j.leaqua.2009.09.006.

Hassan, Arif, and Forbis Ahmed. 2011. "Authentic Leadership, Trust, and Work Engagement." *International Journal of Human and Social Sciences* 6 (3): 164–70.

Helland, Martha R., and Bruce E. Winston. 2005. "Towards a Deeper Understanding of Hope and Leadership." *Journal of Leadership & Organizational Studies* 12 (2): 42–54. https://doi.org/10.1177/107179190501200204.

Highsmith, Jim. 2009. *Agile Project Management: Creating Innovative Products*. 2nd ed. Addison-Wesley.

Hill, Linda A. 2010. "Leading from Behind." *Harvard Business Review* 14: 33–41.

Hudson, F. M. 1999. *The Handbook of Developmental Leadership: A Comprehensive Resource Guide for Managers, Executives, Consultants, and Human Resource Professionals*. Jossey-Bass.

Hughes, David J., Allan Lee, Amy Wei Tian, Alex Newman, and Alison Legood. 2018. "Leadership, Creativity, and Innovation: A Critical Review and Practical Recommendations." *The Leadership Quarterly* 29 (5): 549–69. https://doi.org/10.1016/j.leaqua.2018.03.001.

Keller, Helen. 1999. *The Story of My Life*. (originally published 1903). Dover Publications.

Kloppenborg, Timothy J., and Joseph A. Petrick. 2002. *Managing Project Quality*. Management Concepts.

Kloppenborg, Timothy J., Vittal Anantatmula, and Kathryn N. Wells. 2023. *Contemporary Project Management*. 5th ed. Southwestern/Cengage Learning.

Kolb, David A. 2014. *Experiential Learning: Experience as the Source of Learning and Development*. Pearson FT Press.

Laloux, Frederic. 2014. *Reinventing Organizations: A Guide to Creating Organizations Inspired by the Next Stage of Human Consciousness*. Parker.

Ledesma, Janet. 2014. "Conceptual Frameworks and Research Models on Resilience in Leadership." *SAGE Open* 4 (3): 1–8. https://doi.org/10.1177/2158244014545464.

Mandela, Nelson. 1994. *Long Walk to Freedom: The Autobiography of Nelson Mandela*. Little, Brown & Co.

Norman, Steven M., Bruce J. Avolio, and Fred Luthans. 2010. "The Impact of Positivity and Transparency on Trust in Leaders and Their Perceived Effectiveness." *The Leadership Quarterly* 21 (3): 350–64. https://doi.org/10.1016/j.leaqua.2010.03.002.

Palanski, Michael E., and Francis J. Yammarino. 2009. "Integrity and Leadership: A Multi-Level Conceptual Framework." *The Leadership Quarterly* 20 (3): 405–20. https://doi.org/10.1016/j.leaqua.2009.03.008.

Rego, A., F. Sousa, C. Marques, and M. P. e Cunha. 2014. "Hope and Positive Affect Mediating the Authentic Leadership and Creativity Relationship." *Journal of Business Research* 67 (2): 200–210. https://doi.org/10.1016/j.jbusres.2012.10.003.

Reichard, Rebecca J., James B. Avey, Shane Lopez, and Maren Dollwet. 2013. "Having the Will and Finding the Way: A Review and Meta-Analysis of Hope at Work." *The Journal of Positive Psychology* 8 (4): 292–304. https://doi.org/10.1080/17439760.2013.800903.

Searle, T. P., and J. E. Barbuto Jr. 2011. "Servant Leadership, Hope, and Organizational Virtuousness: A Framework Exploring Positive Micro and Macro Behaviors and Performance Impact." *Journal of Leadership & Organizational Studies* 18 (1): 107-117. 107–117. https://doi.org/10.1177/1548051810383863.

Senge, Peter. 1990. *The Fifth Discipline: The Art and Practice of the Learning Organization.* Doubleday.

Sinek, Simon. 2014. *Leaders Eat Last: Why Some Teams Pull Together and Others Don't.* Portfolio/Penguin.

Snyder, C. Richard. 2002. "Hope Theory: Rainbows in the Mind." *Psychological Inquiry* 13 (4): 249–75. https://doi.org/10.1207/S15327965PLI1304_01.

Sutherland, Jeff, and John Sutherland. 2015. *Scrum: The Art of Doing Twice the Work in Half the Time.* Crown Business.

Trinity Communications. 2024. "Compendium of the Social Doctrine of the Church: Chapter Four." Last modified 2024. https://www.catholicculture.org/culture/library/view.cfm?id=7214#PartIV.

Tuckman, Bruce W. 1965. "Developmental Sequence in Small Groups." *Psychological Bulletin* 63 (6): 384–99. https://doi.org/10.1037/h0022100.

von Krogh, Georg. 1998. "Care in Knowledge Creation." *California Management Review* 40 (3): 133–53.

Wells, Kathryn N., and Timothy J. Kloppenborg. 2019. *Project Management Essentials.* 2nd ed. Business Expert Press.

Winston, Bruce E., and Kathleen Patterson. 2003. "An Integrative Definition of Leadership." International Journal of Leadership Studies 1, no. 2 (2003): 6–66. https://www.regent.edu/acad/global/publications/ijls/new/vol1iss2/winston_patterson.htm

Youssef, C. M., and Fred Luthans. 2007. "Positive Organizational Behavior in the Workplace: The Impact of Hope, Optimism, and Resilience." *Journal of Management* 33 (5): 774–800. https://doi.org/10.1177/0149206307305562.

Bibliography

Anantatmula, V. S. 2024. *Project Teams: A Structured Development Approach.* 2nd ed. Business Expert Press.

IMS. 2019. "Creating Hope." *IMS Blog.* September 23, 2019. Accessed January 13, 2025. https://blog.ims-online.com/index.php/2019/09/23/creating-hope/.

Kloppenborg, Timothy J., and Laurence J. Laning. 2012. *Strategic Leadership of Portfolio and Project Management.* New York: Business Expert Press.

Kloppenborg, Timothy J., Arthur Shriberg, and Jayashree Venkatraman. 2003. *Project Leadership.* New York: Business Expert Press.

Kucia, J. C., and L. S. Gravett. 2014. *Leadership in Balance: New Habits of the Mind.* Palgrave Macmillan.

Maxwell, J. C. 1998. *The 21 Irrefutable Laws of Leadership: Follow Them and People Will Follow You.* Thomas Nelson Publishers.

Worsley, L. M. 2020. *Stakeholder-led Project Management: Changing the Way We Manage Projects.* Business Expert Press.

About the Authors

Timothy J. Kloppenborg is a Professor Emeritus from Xavier University. He has written 15 books—mostly on project management and leadership. Tim's early work after his MBA was on elevator installation and jet engine research projects. He holds a PhD in operations management from the University of Cincinnati. He is a Project Management Professional (PMP), an Agile Certified Professional (ACP), and a Disciplined Agile Senior Scrum Master (DASSM). He started the portfolio and project management book collection for Business Expert Press and edited 70 books in 10 years. Dr. Kloppenborg retired as a major in the U.S. Air Force Reserve. He has trained, taught, and consulted on six continents, most recently serving as Scrum Master for the Heritage Arboretum in Cincinnati, OH.

linkedin.com/in/timkloppenborg

Kam Jugdev is Full Professor in the Faculty of Business at Athabasca University, Alberta, Canada. She holds a joint PhD in Project Management from Schulich School of Engineering and the Haskayne School of Business, University of Calgary and is a Project Management Professional (PMP). She had broad industry experience before her academic career. She teaches project management courses at the undergraduate and graduate levels and enjoys working with graduate research students and research friends. Her research program spans project management as a source of competitive advantage, lessons learned, tools and techniques, and project success/failure.

linkedin.com/in/kamjugdev
Kam Jugdev—Google Scholar

Index

www.ingramcontent.com/pod-product-compliance
Lightning Source LLC
Chambersburg PA
CBHW061321220326
41599CB00026B/4972